READINGS ON

THE GRAPES OF WRATH

OTHER TITLES IN THE GREENHAVEN PRESS LITERARY COMPANION SERIES:

AMERICAN AUTHORS

Maya Angelou
Stephen Crane
Emily Dickinson
William Faulkner
F. Scott Fitzgerald
Nathaniel Hawthorne
Ernest Hemingway
Herman Melville
Arthur Miller
Eugene O'Neill
Edgar Allan Poe
John Steinbeck
Mark Twain
Thornton Wilder

AMERICAN LITERATURE

The Adventures of
  Huckleberry Finn
The Adventures of Tom
  Sawyer
The Call of the Wild
The Catcher in the Rye
The Crucible
Death of a Salesman
The Glass Menagerie
The Great Gatsby
Of Mice and Men
The Old Man and the Sea
The Pearl
The Scarlet Letter
A Separate Peace

BRITISH AUTHORS

Jane Austen
Joseph Conrad
Charles Dickens

BRITISH LITERATURE

Animal Farm
The Canterbury Tales
Great Expectations
Hamlet
Julius Caesar
Lord of the Flies
Macbeth
Pride and Prejudice
Romeo and Juliet
Shakespeare: The Comedies
Shakespeare: The Histories
Shakespeare: The Sonnets
Shakespeare: The Tragedies
A Tale of Two Cities
Wuthering Heights

WORLD AUTHORS

Fyodor Dostoyevsky
Homer
Sophocles

WORLD LITERATURE

All Quiet on the Western
  Front
The Diary of a Young Girl

THE GREENHAVEN PRESS
Literary Companion
TO AMERICAN LITERATURE

READINGS ON

THE GRAPES OF WRATH

David L. Bender, *Publisher*

Bruno Leone, *Executive Editor*

Brenda Stalcup, *Managing Editor*

Bonnie Szumski, *Series Editor*

Gary Wiener, *Book Editor*

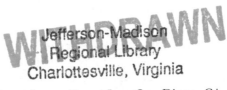
Greenhaven Press, Inc., San Diego, CA

1657 4186

L

Every effort has been made to trace the owners of copyrighted material. The articles in this volume may have been edited for content, length, and/or reading level. The titles have been changed to enhance the editorial purpose. Those interested in locating the original source will find the complete citation on the first page of each article.

Library of Congress Cataloging-in-Publication Data

Readings on The grapes of wrath / Gary Wiener, book editor.
        p.   cm. — (The Greenhaven Press literary
    companion to American literature)
        Includes bibliographical references and index.
        ISBN 1-56510-955-4 (lib. bdg. : alk. paper). —
    ISBN 1-56510-954-6 (pbk. : alk. paper)
        1. Steinbeck, John , 1902–1968. Grapes of wrath.
    2. Migrant agricultural laborers in literature. 3. Labor
    camps in literature. 4. California—In literature.
    I. Wiener, Gary. II. Series.
    PS3537.T3234G887   1999
    813'.52—dc21   98-17684
                                                              CIP

Cover photo: Photofest

Copyright ©1999 by Greenhaven Press, Inc.
PO Box 289009
San Diego, CA 92198-9009
Printed in the U.S.A.

❝I tried to write this book the way lives are being lived not the way books are written.❞

—*John Steinbeck on*
The Grapes of Wrath

CONTENTS

Chapter 1: The Making of the Novel

Though Steinbeck wrote *The Grapes of Wrath* in one hundred
days in 1938, he had written many previous pieces on Oklahoma refugees and the problem of migrant farmworkers in
California. Completing *The Grapes of Wrath* left Steinbeck so
worn-out that he never returned to the novel's subject.

Steinbeck felt that the title *The Grapes of Wrath,* suggested
by his wife Carol, was a perfect choice. He was so excited by
the title that he wrote to his publisher to make sure all of
the lyrics to "The Battle Hymn of the Republic" and, if possible, the musical score were printed in his novel.

The Harvest Gypsies was the name Steinbeck gave to a series of investigative reports about the Okies that he wrote
for a San Francisco newspaper. Steinbeck's account of their
terrible living and working conditions as well as the
hypocrisy of those who hired them is vivid and powerful.

The ending of *The Grapes of Wrath* has been controversial
almost from the moment Steinbeck wrote it. But Steinbeck
rejected alternative endings that were too dependent on government cures or Marxist ideology.

Chapter 2: Major Themes in *The Grapes of Wrath*

Tom Joad belongs to the epic tradition of heroes. Given momentum by the twin forces of Ma Joad and Jim Casy, Tom becomes a true hero for the twentieth century.

Chapter 3: Techniques

stricken people of the 1980s, modern counterparts of the models for Steinbeck's characters fifty years before. Steinbeck told the "hard truth" back then, and his message remains true to this day.

FOREWORD

"'Tis the good reader that
makes the good book."

Ralph Waldo Emerson

The story's bare facts are simple: The captain, an old and scarred seafarer, walks with a peg leg made of whale ivory. He relentlessly drives his crew to hunt the world's oceans for the great white whale that crippled him. After a long search, the ship encounters the whale and a fierce battle ensues. Finally the captain drives his harpoon into the whale, but the harpoon line catches the captain about the neck and drags him to his death.

A simple story, a straightforward plot—yet, since the 1851 publication of Herman Melville's *Moby-Dick*, readers and critics have found many meanings in the struggle between Captain Ahab and the whale. To some, the novel is a cautionary tale that depicts how Ahab's obsession with revenge leads to his insanity and death. Others believe that the whale represents the unknowable secrets of the universe and that Ahab is a tragic hero who dares to challenge fate by attempting to discover this knowledge. Perhaps Melville intended Ahab as a criticism of Americans' tendency to become involved in well-intentioned but irrational causes. Or did Melville model Ahab after himself, letting his fictional character express his anger at what he perceived as a cruel and distant god?

Although literary critics disagree over the meaning of *Moby-Dick*, readers do not need to choose one particular interpretation in order to gain an understanding of Melville's

10

novel. Instead, by examining various analyses, they can gain numerous insights into the issues that lie under the surface of the basic plot. Studying the writings of literary critics can also aid readers in making their own assessments of *Moby-Dick* and other literary works and in developing analytical thinking skills.

The Greenhaven Literary Companion Series was created with these goals in mind. Designed for young adults, this unique anthology series provides an engaging and comprehensive introduction to literary analysis and criticism. The essays included in the Literary Companion Series are chosen for their accessibility to a young adult audience and are expertly edited in consideration of both the reading and comprehension levels of this audience. In addition, each essay is introduced by a concise summation that presents the contributing writer's main themes and insights. Every anthology in the Literary Companion Series contains a varied selection of critical essays that cover a wide time span and express diverse views. Wherever possible, primary sources are represented through excerpts from authors' notebooks, letters, and journals and through contemporary criticism.

Each title in the Literary Companion Series pays careful consideration to the historical context of the particular author or literary work. In-depth biographies and detailed chronologies reveal important aspects of authors' lives and emphasize the historical events and social milieu that influenced their writings. To facilitate further research, every anthology includes primary and secondary source bibliographies of articles and/or books selected for their suitability for young adults. These engaging features make the Greenhaven Literary Companion series ideal for introducing students to literary analysis in the classroom or as a library resource for young adults researching the world's great authors and literature.

Exceptional in its focus on young adults, the Greenhaven Literary Companion Series strives to present literary criticism in a compelling and accessible format. Every title in the series is intended to spark readers' interest in leading American and world authors, to help them broaden their understanding of literature, and to encourage them to formulate their own analyses of the literary works that they read. It is the editors' hope that young adult readers will find these anthologies to be true companions in their study of literature.

INTRODUCTION

The publication of *The Grapes of Wrath* in 1939 remains a pivotal event in the life and writing career of John Steinbeck. Steinbeck is well known for many books, including *The Red Pony, Cannery Row, East of Eden, Of Mice and Men,* and *The Pearl.* In many ways, however, all of his other works flow up to and surge away from the writing of his "big book," as Steinbeck often referred to *The Grapes of Wrath.* It is his magnum opus, the "Great American Novel" that so many authors strive all of their lives to produce. In the words of one of Steinbeck's most influential critics, Peter Lisca, *The Grapes of Wrath* "is unquestionably John Steinbeck's finest achievement, a work of literary genius."

Yet, over the years there has been much debate as to whether *The Grapes of Wrath* is an important book, a great work of art, or both. The Pulitzer and Nobel prizes accorded to Steinbeck would seem to argue for both. So too, would the novel's continuing endurance, its secure place on high school and college reading lists, and its wide audience. It is a book that focuses on a particular people, the Oklahoman dust bowl refugees, or "Okies" as they were known, at a particular point in time, the Great Depression of the 1930s. But like most great works, the novel has a universal message that reaches far beyond place and time. As Mimi Reisel Gladstein suggests, "while the immigrant's experience can be categorized on a personal level and also be seen as a national paradigm, it is not just in America that *The Grapes of Wrath* endures. Steinbeck's pages communicate to a world-wide audience."

From the beginning, Steinbeck knew that he was onto something: "If only I could do this book properly it would be one of the really fine books and a truly American book," he wrote in his diary. Though he was assailed throughout the course of writing the novel by self-doubt and fears of his own inadequacy ("I'm not a writer," another diary entry reads,

"I've been fooling myself and other people"), it is clear that his first impulse was correct. The novel that emerged after a one-hundred-day marathon of writing was everything Steinbeck believed it could be and more.

For its social significance, its effect on an entire country's attitudes, *The Grapes of Wrath* ranks with Harriet Beecher Stowe's exposé of slavery, *Uncle Tom's Cabin,* and Upton Sinclair's similarly powerful attack on the meat packing industry, *The Jungle.* For its philosophical and artistic expressions of America at a particular point in its history, it finds a place in the American literary canon of novels that includes *The Scarlet Letter, Moby-Dick, The Great Gatsby,* and *Native Son.* Even a noted Steinbeck detractor such as Yale professor Harold Bloom acknowledges that "no canonical standards worthy of human respect could exclude *The Grapes of Wrath* from a serious reader's esteem."

Readings on The Grapes of Wrath has several special features that will appeal to young readers. A synopsis appears at the beginning of each article. The articles have been edited for readability, with in-text explanations of difficult allusions and concepts. Articles have also been edited so that each covers one major thread—digressions and particularly obtuse reflections have been cut. The reader will also find, interspersed with the essays, inserts that expand, supplement, and augment the reader's experience of *The Grapes of Wrath.*

Although Steinbeck's reputation certainly ebbed during his last decade and for many years that followed, the more recent essays recognize the greatness of the novel and of the author's vision.

JOHN STEINBECK: A BIOGRAPHY

How surprised John Steinbeck's parents might have been had they lived long enough to see him become an immensely famous, major American author. At the time of their deaths, within fifteen months of each other, Steinbeck was an unemployed dropout of Stanford University. Though he was a published author, his earnings were meager, and he was still collecting a monthly allowance from his father. In many ways, Steinbeck's life is a study in contradictions. He made his career championing the poor and downtrodden, but came to prefer the company of Hollywood's rich and famous. Though much of his work found a large audience and continues to be read and studied in high school and college literature courses, he was scorned by literary critics for years. Steinbeck was awarded the Nobel Prize in literature in 1962 even as such critical condemnation reached its peak.

John Ernst Steinbeck III was the third of four children of John Ernst Steinbeck II and his wife, the former Olive Hamilton. Born on February 27, 1902, he was their only boy, sandwiched among three sisters. The Steinbeck family lived in Salinas, California, at the north end of a valley thirty miles inland from the Pacific Ocean. Salinas is the seat of Monterey County, of which Steinbeck's father was the treasurer for many years. This "long valley" has long been one of America's most productive agricultural regions, with lettuce, celery, beets, fruit, and grain as its major crops. The Salinas Valley and California in general would play a major role in Steinbeck's work, and he would later satirize the area as "Lettuceberg."

The Steinbecks have been described as "definitely bourgeois," or middle class, but the family's status was enhanced because they lived in a large Victorian house and were active in the community. John Ernst Steinbeck II managed a flour mill; Olive Steinbeck had been a teacher in a one-room schoolhouse.

MAMA'S BOY

In his earliest years Steinbeck, who was rather homely with oversized ears and pointed features, was considered by others a shy mama's boy. After two daughters, Olive Steinbeck longed for an educable boy, for whom she held high ambitions. She knew that, at least at the turn of the century, the best that education and culture could provide for her daughters was a teaching position. As a former schoolteacher, Olive was determined that all of her children be versed in the arts, so she read to all of them. To John, she read fairy tales at two, passages from the Bible and animal stories at three, and such tales as *Treasure Island, Robin Hood,* and *Ivanhoe* a year later. By five John was reading simple tales himself.

At six, he entered elementary school, or "Baby School," as it was termed in Salinas, advanced in reading and writing, but limited socially by his plain looks and lack of self-confidence. His mother's overprotectiveness caused friction between Olive and her husband, who believed that she had made him weak and vulnerable in a world where a young man needed to be strong. His father attempted to school his son in what he considered to be more manly fields: farming, gardening, and country life.

In third grade, caught between his shyness and the need to be more social, John became difficult in class. He began causing trouble, which necessitated a number of parent conferences. While Olive considered such behavior shameful, the elder Steinbeck evidently read such outbursts as the not completely objectionable result of his training. John eventually settled down.

At this time John often spent weekends with his Aunt Molly, his mother's sister, on her ranch west of Salinas. Molly immersed the boy in cultural activities, which included listening to music, reading passages from the classics, and writing. "It was education by osmosis," Steinbeck would later say. "I couldn't stand it. I grew to hate it, grew to hate my aunt and dread those visits with her. I wanted to be out roaming the pastures and she had trapped me in a prison of words." It was Molly who first introduced Steinbeck to *Le Morte d'Arthur,* the tales of Camelot and the Arthurian round table by Sir Thomas Malory that would figure in so many of his later works, from *Tortilla Flat* to *Sweet Thursday.*

AN INTEREST IN WRITING

Steinbeck's early high school career could hardly be called distinguished. He had few friends, was seldom motivated in his studies, and rarely applied himself fully to his school-work. But during his freshman year, he decided that he would be a writer. Years later, he described his early efforts:

> I used to sit in that little room upstairs . . . and write little sto-ries and little pieces and send them out to magazines under a false name and I never knew what happened to them because I never put a return address on them. But I would watch the magazines for a certain length of time to see whether they had printed them. They never did because they couldn't get in touch with me. . . . I wonder what I was thinking of? I was scared to death to get a rejection slip, but more, I suppose, to get an acceptance.

Eventually, his parents came to fear that he was spending too much time in his room writing, to the exclusion of his studies. They hoped to send him to nearby Stanford University and feared that his grades might be inadequate for admission. At this time Steinbeck discovered another lifelong interest, science. A friend's father was an ornithologist at Stanford's oceanographic laboratory, and the young Steinbeck spent long hours with the scientist, watching as he labeled specimens and prepared them for display.

In the spring of his junior year, Steinbeck contracted a cold that developed into pleurisy, an infection of the membrane that surrounds the lungs, and pneumonia. He became gravely ill; finally, as a last resort, a doctor removed a rib, allowing the pus that had collected below to drain. He lay in a coma for several days, then began to recover.

Steinbeck's brush with death appeared to have made him a more serious young man when he finally returned to school. In his senior year he edited the school yearbook, *El Gabilan,* and was voted class president. Lest one think of him as a suddenly outgoing, charismatic politician, however, consider the words of biographer Jackson J. Benson, who writes of his high school years:

> Salinas High School had at that time only twenty-four gradu-ating seniors. . . . While the election of John Steinbeck as se-nior class president . . . suggests that he was a very popular, socially active boy, just the opposite was true. Members of the class cannot remember him as president and in retrospect can't think how, considering his shyness and lack of popular-ity, he could have been elected. He did not have any really close friends in high school.

The summer after his high school graduation, Steinbeck took a job as a laborer to make money to attend college after his wealthy aunt, Molly, who had promised to help put the Steinbeck children through college, died. Her husband remarried and reneged on the offer. He found himself among men with whom he had never had much contact—Mexican, Chinese, and other unskilled immigrants who made up Monterey County's common labor force. He liked and fit in with his fellow workers, who jovially called the former mama's boy "Johnny boy" and exposed him to the unrefined side of life that he would later feature in so many of his works. But numerous newspaper and magazine articles that he read that summer condemned these migrants. Disturbed by the mistaken impression, Steinbeck dashed off a letter to a San Francisco newspaper, which went unpublished but which foreshadows his defense of such workers in *The Grapes of Wrath:*

> I have worked with the men your article described for well over a month now and I can tell you that fellow who wrote it is living in a fairyland. . . . These men are outgoing and generous and surly and fractious, often happy with their lot, sometimes ill-tempered and nasty . . . all in all just like a lot of people I know who work in white collars and green eyeshades.

IN AND OUT OF STANFORD UNIVERSITY

Steinbeck enrolled in Stanford, one of the premier universities in the country, in October 1919. He attended school sporadically until the spring of 1925, hampered by a lack of interest in his studies, illness, and a general disdain for college. Instead of applying himself to his studies, he would write stories, wander about campus, roam the nearby countryside, and indulge in a number of less acceptable activities, such as drinking and carousing. He continually fell behind in his studies, and labored unsuccessfully to catch up. Years later, upon experiencing difficulty with *The Grapes of Wrath*, he would write, "It's just like slipping behind at Stanford. Panic sets in. Can't organize."

On several occasions during these years, Steinbeck dropped out of school, finding work at a series of jobs that more often than not involved manual labor. Above all, he now knew he wanted to be a writer, and he would often read his works to his roommate and good friend, George Mors, who offered constructive criticism. But convincing his parents his goal was worthy was not easy. They were frustrated by his lack of success at college, and though his father continually helped him by getting the younger Steinbeck work or giving him money, he found his son's behavior something of an embarrassment. Returning to school in 1924, Steinbeck began to gain some writing success at Stanford, publishing stories in the school newspaper and developing a reputation around campus as a writer. Later he would say he spent this period inventing himself as a series of different characters, all artificial poses in an effort to convince others that he was a writer. Steinbeck was again supported by a friend, a fellow English major named Duke Sheffield, who also wanted to become a writer. Toward the end of his final stay at college, encouraged by a professor, Steinbeck began to expand one of his short stories, "The Lady in Infra-Red," about an eighteenth-century pirate named Henry Morgan. Soon he had forty pages of a novel he called *Pot of Gold*. But his schoolwork suffered again, and he knew he was finally finished at Stanford. Encouraged by his father, he doubled the length of his manuscript during the summer, but the work soon bogged down, and Steinbeck, feeling that he lacked the worldly experience to write such a work, set off to the literary capital of the United States, New York City, where his older, now married sister, Elizabeth, lived.

BECOMING A NOVELIST

In New York, Steinbeck worked in construction and then landed a job with the *American*, a Hearst newspaper. He used his Stanford contacts to interest an editor in his short stories, but by the time he prepared an entire book's worth, the editor had taken another job and no one else would seriously consider the work of an unknown. Steinbeck also had a brief romance with a showgirl, but when she tried to talk him into leaving writing for a more "serious" career, the affair ended. Having neglected the duties of his job at the *American* for writing and romance, he was first demoted and then fired. He soon returned to California.

Steinbeck obtained a job as caretaker of a wealthy widow's estate near Lake Tahoe and continued writing. In a letter he wrote two years later, Steinbeck describes this time as one of great personal growth, during which he outgrew the artificial selves he had fashioned at Stanford:

> I went into the mountains and stayed two years. I was snowed in eight months of the year and saw no one. . . . And there was no one to pose for anymore. You can't have a show with no audience. Gradually all the poses slipped off and when I came out of the hills I didn't have any poses anymore.

In 1927 *Smoker's Companion* accepted his story "The Gifts of Ivan," which he submitted under the pseudonym of John Stern. At twenty-five, John Steinbeck had published his first work. In February 1928 he finally finished the manuscript *Pot of Gold*, but completion of the work seemed only to discourage him. Almost afraid to revise it, he brought the text to his former Stanford professors, Elizabeth Smith and Edith Mirrielees, who encouraged him to attempt publication. Smith suggested the title *Cup of Gold*. Publishers would not consider a manuscript written in longhand, however, so when a vacationing secretary named Carol Henning offered to type it for him, he accepted. Henning believed in the book, and in John as well, and refused to accept money for the job. The two were soon dating, and in January 1929, *Cup of Gold* was accepted for publication.

He still struggled to find his voice, his themes, and his plots, and often felt caught between romantic tales of high adventure fashioned after the Arthurian stories he loved so much, and those of the common people he knew and understood from his various stints as a laborer. But when Steinbeck was able to combine the two impulses, his career blossomed. Over the next decade he would produce much of his most highly acclaimed work. Having been interested in philosophy and biology since his high school days, Steinbeck wondered about and wrestled with several profound issues in his writing: What was the individual's place in society? Were humans caught between their base animal urges and the rational dictates of their minds? And why were there so many poor and hungry people in a land of plenty?

With the stock market crash of 1929 and the subsequent depression of the thirties, Steinbeck's career suffered as much as any other worker's. He completed a novel, *To an Unknown God*, and submitted it for publication, but the book was rejected by the press that had published *Cup of Gold* as well as a succession of other publishers. Steinbeck was surprised: for him *To an Unknown God* represented a significant improvement over *Cup*, which he felt he had outgrown even before the novel appeared in print. But the depression was already taking its toll. At least one publisher rejected *To an Unknown God* with the admission that in a better financial climate, it might have been accepted.

Steinbeck grew more serious about Carol Henning, who continued to type his manuscripts. As Robert DeMott writes, "She too was an energetic, talented person—among other things, a versifier, satirist, prose writer, painter, caricaturist— who agreed to relinquish a possible career in favor of helping to manage his. It seems to have been a partnership based more on reciprocal need and shared affection than on deep romantic love." They were married on January 14, 1930. Carol worked as a secretary, and Steinbeck's father, impressed that his son was a published novelist, supplemented their income with $25 a month. But Steinbeck, ever aware of his inability to provide, suffered through periods of depression as he neared the age of thirty without having found a career that could pay his bills, convinced if he did not make it as a self-sufficient writer soon, he would be too old to undertake any other type of life's work.

A host of other problems confronted the Steinbecks. Carol entered into business dealings that failed. Steinbeck had neglected his teeth for years and endured increasing dental pain. The repair he needed cost more than he could afford, and so each time he came into some modest sum he submitted to a portion of the work. While visiting his dentist in the fall of 1930, Steinbeck met a man who was to have a major impact on his life and work. Edward F. Ricketts, five years older than Steinbeck and a marine biologist by trade, was a brilliant, quirky loner who founded Pacific Biological Laboratories in the section of Monterey along the waterfront known as Cannery Row. The company collected and labeled marine specimens, which it sold to other labs and universities. Steinbeck became an almost daily visitor to Ricketts's lab. He watched the scientist work and engaged in long discussions on everything from the scientific method to fiction writing.

In 1932 Steinbeck's friend Carl Wilhelmson suggested that instead of using the part-time services of his New York agent, Ted Miller, Steinbeck should consider full-time literary agents. Mavis McIntosh and Elizabeth Otis agreed to represent Steinbeck and soon sold *Pastures of Heaven* to Jonathan Cape and Harrison Smith, an American subsidiary of a well-known British publishing house. Reviews of the novel were poor. Suffering from financial woes, Cape and Smith afterward withdrew an offer to publish future Steinbeck works.

EARLY SUCCESSES

In May 1932 Steinbeck's mother suffered a stroke. During this time he and Carol moved back to the family home in Salinas to care for his mother and father, while Steinbeck continued working on *To an Unknown God.* He continued his friendship with Ed Ricketts, who was becoming a major influence on Steinbeck's thought and work. At Ricketts's suggestion, Steinbeck retitled his novel *To a God Unknown*, and it was published by Cape and Smith when the firm's finances improved.

Elizabeth Otis, who at this time handled only his short fiction, sold his story "The Red Pony," which appeared in two installments in the prestigious *North American Review*. While the money was negligible, the exposure was substantial. The publication of "The Red Pony" gained him a following he had not attained despite his three published novels. The *North American Review* next published "The Murder," which would win the O. Henry Award as the best short story of 1934.

At Ed Ricketts's suggestion, Steinbeck began writing about the *paisanos*, or poor Mexicans, of Monterey. These stories were to become the novel *Tortilla Flat*, which he completed just before Olive Steinbeck died in February 1934. His mother's death, after prolonged illness, was more a relief than a shock, and Steinbeck spent little time in mourning.

A short story written in the spring of that year, "The Raid," was also the product of Steinbeck's long conversations with Ricketts. The piece was published by the *North American Review* in the summer of 1934. "The Raid" was the story of an aging communist labor organizer and his young protégé, and its success led to a similar, longer tale about the labor crisis in California that Steinbeck would call *In Dubious Battle*, after a line from John Milton's epic poem, *Paradise Lost*.

Despite the success of his short fiction, *Tortilla Flat* had unsuccessfully made the rounds of publishing houses. Steinbeck, who usually lost interest in a manuscript once he finished writing it and who was rarely impressed by seeing his books in print, had all but dismissed the novel as a failed exercise while immersing himself in *In Dubious Battle*.

Thus it was something of a surprise when, in January 1935, the publishing house of Covici-Friede offered not only to publish *Tortilla Flat* but to reissue his previous novels and become his exclusive publisher. Pascal "Pat" Covici had been visiting a Chicago bookseller who had been tremendously impressed by Steinbeck's work in the *North American Review*. The bookseller recommended that Covici read *Pastures of Heaven*. Covici loved the novel. Steinbeck's circle of influential friends who would greatly help his career was now complete: Pat Covici, his publisher; Elizabeth Otis, his literary agent; and Ed Ricketts, his mentor and fellow philosopher.

Right away there were problems, however. Covici was

skeptical about publishing *In Dubious Battle*, believing, with good reason, that it would be attacked from both the right and the left for its treatment of labor unionism in California. But Elizabeth Otis convinced Covici that, whatever its politics, *In Dubious Battle* was a highly marketable book. From this point on, Otis would become the principal literary agent for all of Steinbeck's work.

Covici-Friede brought out *Tortilla Flat* in May 1935. The novel that Steinbeck had dismissed as unimportant took the country by storm. Steinbeck's father, who had been ailing since his wife's stroke, died days before its publication, just as his son would begin to gain national attention. Steinbeck would never again have to worry about money. On top of his inheritance, *Tortilla Flat* began to bring in something his other books had never earned: royalty checks. Suddenly the writer who had been living on an allowance from his father was wealthy, especially after Otis sold the movie rights to the novel for $4,000, a substantial sum during the Great Depression. John and Carol's marriage had suffered from their relative poverty, the stress of his parents' illnesses, and his immersion in his work. With their newfound wealth they traveled to Mexico, ostensibly on vacation, but also to repair their marriage.

Covici had been right about *In Dubious Battle*; upon its publication, the novel caused a political uproar, and its literary qualities were largely ignored. Nevertheless, it sold well. In the spring of 1936 Steinbeck was already hard at work on his next project, the novella he would call, at Ricketts's suggestion, *Of Mice and Men*. This story concerns two migrant workers, George and Lennie, who seek a home of their own. To give it the dramatic qualities he wanted, Steinbeck conceived of it as a play in prose. After the great success of this novella, he would try to repeat this formula many times, with varying degrees of success, in his later works.

PLANNING THE BIG NOVEL

In response to Steinbeck's growing status as a writer, and because of his reputation as a chronicler of the lower classes, the *San Francisco News* asked him to research and write a series of articles on the growing migrant worker problem in California. What Steinbeck saw appalled him. The migrants endured horrific working and living conditions, and widespread strikes and rebellions were often the result. Entire families lived on diets of dandelion greens and boiled potatoes; workers earned pennies a day and were charged excessive amounts for food; hospitals turned away to die sick migrants who lacked money to pay doctor's fees.

A government-run camp for migrants known as Weedpatch was among the few promising sights Steinbeck observed. The camp was run by Thomas Collins, a government employee. The two quickly became friends, and it is Collins whose name appears in the dedication to *The Grapes of Wrath:* "To Tom, who lived it." But that big novel, the magnum opus that Steinbeck for years had dreamed of producing, was still a dream.

Already his interest in the migrants was causing controversy. Some blamed *In Dubious Battle* for inciting workers. The *San Francisco News* delayed publication of the articles it had commissioned for fear that their anticorporate stance would alienate potential advertisers. This delay angered Steinbeck, who resolved to write a sequel to *In Dubious Battle* that would focus on the lives of the exploited workers. "The subject is so huge that it scares me to death," he wrote to Otis. He made what might best be described as a false start in a manuscript he satirically titled "L'Affaire Lettuceberg." According to biographer Kenneth Ferrell, "Steinbeck wanted to write movingly about the plight of the migrants, a big book with a big theme. Instead, he found himself producing a short satire, bitter and sophomoric." He would later burn the seventy-thousand-word manuscript.

Meanwhile, *Of Mice and Men,* published in February 1937, and was an immediate best-seller and Book-of-the-Month Club choice, bringing Steinbeck more money than he had earned in his entire lifetime. With "Lettuceberg" coming along badly, the Steinbecks used some of their windfall to travel first to New York and then to Europe. In New York Steinbeck found himself a celebrity, welcomed at all the best parties and celebrated in the New York papers. But he quickly tired of fame. Overwhelmed by the attention, Steinbeck felt his shyness reemerge; he bored most of the other celebrities and they bored him. "I was not made for success," he wrote. "In many ways it is a terrible thing. . . . Among other things I feel as if I have put something over. That this little success of mine is cheating."

In New York, Steinbeck worked with the highly successful director and playwright George Kaufman on turning *Of Mice and Men* into a play. Then he and Carol left for Europe, which he enjoyed, finding Europeans less interested in the

cult of celebrity than Americans. A trip to Russia was somewhat disappointing; the Russians tended to lionize Steinbeck
as a champion of the working classes, but he was not interested in becoming anyone's savior, and subsequently
dropped a plan to write a novel about that country. Returning
to New York, Steinbeck resumed work with George Kaufman,
then left abruptly for California. The play *Of Mice and Men*
opened to stellar reviews, and won the 1937 Drama Critics
Circle Award.

Kaufman was dismayed by Steinbeck's premature departure, but the novelist clearly had his reasons. He and Carol
rented a car and drove cross-country, taking the route that
Oklahoman migrant workers, or "Okies," as they were deri-
sively known, had traveled when dust bowl conditions in the
Midwest forced them from their farms. Steinbeck's big novel
would no longer be set entirely in "Lettuceberg." He planned
an epic, the story of an odyssey that would culminate in California and depict the terrible ordeal so many workers faced
during the depression.

But when Steinbeck returned to California he found that
his fame had preceded him. Autograph seekers, would-be
writers, tourists, and Hollywood producers besieged him at
his home. Carol badly wanted to move to a fifty-acre ranch
west of Los Gatos, but Steinbeck, foreseeing overwhelming
maintenance obligations, was hesitant. Carol prevailed, and
they purchased the ranch in the summer of 1938. Their trip
to Mexico had helped solidify their marriage for a time, but
cracks were again beginning to show.

WRITING *THE GRAPES OF WRATH*

Steinbeck immersed himself in his writing. In an extraordinary one-hundred-day burst between June and October
1938, he hand wrote the two-hundred-thousand-word novel
The Grapes of Wrath. The book is almost universally considered his greatest work. It would ultimately win him the
Pulitzer Prize and form the basis of a career that would be re-
warded with a Nobel Prize, but as usual Steinbeck was less
than confident about its construction. The diary he kept during this period, published in 1989 as *Working Days: The Journals of* The Grapes of Wrath, is full of self-doubt and personal
pep talks, as if Steinbeck did not believe in his own creative
powers. The strain of the undertaking comes across clearly;
on June 20, he wrote: "Must slow down and take it easier . . .
had a feeling of exhaustion near to collapse. I guess I'd been

working too hard. It's not the amount of work but the almost physical drive that goes into it that seems to make the difference." Continually he laments the erratic pace of his writing. "Well, the work has pretty much gone to hell," he wrote on August 8, almost one-hundred-thousand words into the manuscript; "So many things to drive me nuts." His work was continually interrupted by guests and passers-by; Carol had a painful tonsillectomy, which temporarily incapacitated her; his publisher, Covici-Friede, went bankrupt during the summer; the movie director Pare Lorentz wanted to film *In Dubious Battle;* and the duties of the ranch were a constant distraction. "Was ever a book written under such difficulty?" Steinbeck wondered. Even as he neared the finish, his doubts surfaced: "I am sure of one thing—it isn't the great book I had hoped it would be. It's just a run-of-the-mill book. And the awful thing is that it is absolutely the best I can do."

Viking Press had hired Pat Covici, who brought with him Steinbeck's contract. But when Steinbeck sent him Carol's 751-page typescript in December 1938, the editor had his doubts. He was greatly impressed by the work, but, along with other editors at Viking, felt that some of the language and imagery needed softening, particularly in the sexually explicit scene at the end of the novel. Steinbeck believed in the integrity of his work and would not alter it, especially the ending. Viking tried to persuade him to at least introduce the dying man earlier in the manuscript so that he would not be a complete stranger when he is suckled by Rose of Sharon. Steinbeck refused: "The giving of the breast has no more sentiment than the giving of a piece of bread," he argued. Another disagreement stemmed from the title. Carol had suggested *The Grapes of Wrath,* a phrase drawn from "The Battle Hymn of the Republic." Her role in typing the novel, shielding Steinbeck from distractions, and providing critical commentary cannot be underestimated. Certainly Steinbeck did not; one-half of his dedication reads "To CAROL who willed this book." Steinbeck liked her suggestion for the title so much that he wanted all of the lyrics to "The Battle Hymn of the Republic" printed on the endpapers; Covici wanted to print only the verse in which the title phrase appears. Again Steinbeck prevailed; the book was published in 1939 virtually as Steinbeck had written and conceived it.

The novel was an immediate best-seller and would remain so for many months. Not surprisingly, reviews of the controversial work were mixed; most frequently criticized was the ending, which *New Yorker* book critic Clifton Fadiman called "the tawdriest kind of fake symbolism." But Steinbeck never had much use for the critics. He had finally written his big book, and he would stand by it.

AFTERMATH OF THE BIG NOVEL

Writing *The Grapes of Wrath* had taken such a physical and emotional toll on Steinbeck that he would never be quite the same writer or man again. Although his public called for another big, social novel, he occupied himself with a series of lesser projects, and his continued squabbles with Carol would soon lead to their divorce.

Steinbeck became well acquainted with Hollywood and its stars as first *The Grapes of Wrath* and soon after *Of Mice and Men* were made into major motion pictures. Initially skeptical about the Hollywood scene, Steinbeck formed a more favorable opinion based in part on his friendships with actors Spencer Tracy, Henry Fonda and even Charlie Chaplin, who visited the Steinbeck home. But Carol was not fond of Hollywood, and returned to the ranch following another marital dispute. It was at this time that Steinbeck met Gwyndolyn Conger, a young, attractive, aspiring actress, with whom he would soon fall in love.

To put some distance between himself and *The Grapes of Wrath,* Steinbeck conceived of a voyage to Mexico's Baja California peninsula. Ed Ricketts's Pacific Biological Laboratories was near bankruptcy, and Steinbeck, now wealthy beyond his dreams, rescued his friend by purchasing half the stock in the company. The one condition was that the two take this voyage about which Steinbeck would then write a nonfiction account. Happy to have his friend along, Ricketts agreed. Carol, increasingly uneasy about the marriage, insisted on coming along. Steinbeck still maintained hope of restoring his marriage, driven by the knowledge that no one in his family had undergone a divorce. The trip went well, though it did not repair the relationship. Steinbeck spent much of his time in long conversations with Ricketts. While in Mexico, Steinbeck heard a legend about a boy who finds a giant pearl worth a fortune only to find it brings him a series of misfortunes. He would later turn this story into the novella, *The Pearl.*

Arriving back in California, Steinbeck learned that he had won the 1939 Pulitzer Prize in fiction. Even more astounding was the news that First Lady Eleanor Roosevelt had made a

visit to the migrant camps and stated publicly that Steinbeck's account was disturbingly accurate. Her admiration for
Steinbeck would lead to personal meetings between President Roosevelt and the author. Steinbeck went to work on an
account of the Mexican trip that he would call *Sea of Cortez:
A Leisurely Journal of Travel and Research*. Because Ricketts
had so influenced its content and even written some of the
book, Steinbeck would list the authors as John Steinbeck and
Edward F. Ricketts Jr.

World War II had begun in Europe and Steinbeck's attention often turned to global interests. He was eager to confront
the Nazi threat, and made two trips to Washington to discuss
matters with President Roosevelt even before America entered the war. Apparently, though, Steinbeck was granted an
audience only because of Eleanor Roosevelt's great admiration for his work, and Steinbeck's opinions were politely received but largely ignored.

By 1941 Steinbeck's marriage was in shambles. He was
openly living with Gwyndolyn at the Pacific Grove cottage he
had inherited from his parents. Carol had moved to New
York. Steinbeck's lawyers informed him that a divorce would
be costly, so he actively began planning a new book that
could bring in as much money as *Of Mice and Men* or *The
Grapes of Wrath*. Combining two needs, he wrote *The Moon
Is Down*, a critically panned but best-selling story of a Nazi
invasion of California. Among her many demands, Carol
wanted half of all future profits on books he had written
while married to her. Steinbeck agreed. He was eager to
marry Gwyndolyn Conger and start the family he had not
had with Carol.

The divorce from Carol came through in March 1943.
Gwyndolyn presumed that once she and John married, they
would settle down. But Steinbeck was off to London in June
1943 and North Africa in August as a war correspondent for
the New York *Herald-Tribune*. Despite the birth of two sons,
Thom in 1944, and John in 1946, his marriage to Gwyndolyn
was doomed. Even before the marriage, Steinbeck was making numerous trips, some to Hollywood to write propaganda
films for the war effort. These film scripts included *Bombs
Away: The Story of a Bomber Team*, and the classic *Lifeboat*,
on which he worked with the acclaimed director Alfred
Hitchcock.

Upon his return, Steinbeck conceived of a novel about the
denizens of Monterey that he would ultimately publish as

Cannery Row. The novel set out to be another lower-class study, with one important difference. The character of Doc in the novel was clearly based on "the greatest man I have ever known and the best teacher," as Steinbeck would elsewhere write of Ed Ricketts. The plot of the story concerns a group of impoverished squatters in the waterfront area known as Cannery Row. In their own preposterous manner, this motley crew of men plans a party for their friend Doc, who, like Ricketts, is the owner of a biological laboratory. The novel, published early in 1945, was again well received by the public but criticized by reviewers as Steinbeck doing Steinbeck, and not very well, again.

In April 1945 Steinbeck took another trip to Mexico to work on the filming of his script for *The Pearl.* During this time, he formulated the idea for another novel, the story of a busload of traveling Mexicans he was to call *The Wayward Bus.* Having failed to please the critics, and worse, he believed, having written nothing of substance in the six years since *The Grapes of Wrath,* he labored mightily at the novel. Still, he was dissatisfied with the first draft and convinced the work needed substantial revisions. Loath to begin, he instead planned a trip to Scandinavia with Gwyndolyn as another attempt to revive the failing marriage. But Pat Covici did not want a delay in the publishing of the next Steinbeck opus. He knew that anything Steinbeck wrote would be a major seller. So he persuaded the author to publish the novel as it was. Steinbeck agreed, but the premature publication of *The Wayward Bus* (1947) did nothing to alter his perception that his storytelling skills were fading. Though *The Wayward Bus* was another great popular success, Steinbeck's doubts were reinforced, when, after the initial flurry of positive reviews, a few critics found major flaws in the work.

Personal Losses

In 1948, Steinbeck was again commissioned by the New York *Herald-Tribune* to travel to Russia to write about the changes that World War II had wrought on the common people. Few Americans were journeying to Russia at the beginning of the cold war, and Steinbeck was soon pleased to find that he was regarded as something of an expert in international matters. It was a role he was to cultivate for the rest of his career. His articles were later collected as the book *A Russian Journal.*

His marriage continued to deteriorate. Gwyndolyn had begun an affair with a younger man, and when the liaison ended unhappily, she was drinking heavily just as Steinbeck returned from Russia. Then an unexpected event shattered Steinbeck's life. A train had hit Ed Ricketts's car and killed the scientist. His mentor and best friend was gone. Gwyndolyn, who had always resented Ricketts, used the loss as a weapon to put an end to their ill-fated marriage. "Without him you are nothing," she is said to have berated him. "You will now be the failure you were before you met him, and I don't want to be married to a failure." She filed for divorce shortly after, and Steinbeck agreed. Steinbeck's sons went to live with their mother. In the span of a few short months, he had lost his friend, wife, and two sons.

A CAREER IN DECLINE

For a while his only work was a filmscript called *Zapata,* about the Mexican revolutionary. The script would eventually be filmed as *Viva Zapata!,* with renowned actor Marlon Brando in the lead role. But within a year of his divorce Steinbeck met the woman with whom he was to spend the rest of his life. A mutual friend introduced the novelist to Elaine Scott, who was unhappily married to film actor Zachary Scott. The couple married after her divorce from Scott in 1950. Steinbeck went to work on the big historical novel he called *Salinas Valley,* for which he had collected notes for many years. The novel was to be a fictional account of his own family history from the Civil War era on, beginning with his grandfather, Samuel Hamilton. After many abortive attempts, he seriously turned his attention to the book. No doubt he was worried over the effort such an undertaking would require. "I don't want to get too tired," he wrote. "I want to take enough time so that I will avoid the rather terrible exhaustion of *The Grapes of Wrath.*" As he did during the composition of *The Grapes of Wrath,* Steinbeck kept a log of his work on the new novel. On the left-hand side of each page, he wrote a running commentary directed toward Pat Covici. On the right he wrote the novel. Midway through the book, Steinbeck added a second family, the Trasks, to the story of the Hamiltons. As the book began to take on more biblical themes, he also changed the name to *East of Eden,* after a phrase in the Book of Genesis describing Adam and Eve's banishment from the Garden of Eden. Though his editors at Viking advised substantial revisions, Steinbeck refused to make them. The novel was published in the fall of 1952. Again the public embraced the book; again the critics savaged it. Throughout the fifties, this reaction was repeated every time Steinbeck published a book. The novels that followed—*Sweet Thursday*, a rewrite of *Cannery Row; The Short Reign of Pippin IV*, an optimistic tale set in France; and *The Winter of Our Discontent*, a satire about the corruption of good men—were all subjected to harsh criticism. As the critics doubted Steinbeck's storytelling mastery, so too did the novelist begin to lose faith. But his marriage to Elaine remained a source of strength, even when his two sons (teenagers who had become too troublesome for their mother) and her daughter, Waverly, came to live with them and some friction ensued in the household.

Steinbeck became active in Democratic party politics. He championed the presidential candidacies of Adlai Stevenson, who lost twice to Dwight D. Eisenhower, and he was invited to John F. Kennedy's inauguration in 1961. After Kennedy's death, he embraced his successor, Lyndon B. Johnson, and became a regular visitor to the Johnson White House.

In 1962 Steinbeck was awarded the Nobel Prize in literature. At the time, only five other Americans had won the award: Sinclair Lewis, Eugene O'Neill, Pearl Buck, William Faulkner, and Ernest Hemingway. Whatever the critics believed, Steinbeck had been admitted to rarefied literary company. That same year he released the book *Travels with Charley*, an account of his cross-country drive in 1961 with the family french poodle. For once the critics were almost generous, praising the book as a travelogue. It would be his last major work. In 1967 he went to Vietnam to cover the war for the Long Island newspaper *Newsday*. The following year he experienced declining health, enduring back surgery, a stroke, and a series of heart attacks. On December 20, 1968, he suffered a massive heart attack and died at the age of sixty-six. He is buried in Salinas, California.

CHAPTER 1

The Making of the Novel

READINGS ON
THE GRAPES OF WRATH

The Writing of *The Grapes of Wrath*

Robert DeMott

John Steinbeck kept a daily journal during the writing of *The Grapes of Wrath*. In this essay, adapted from the introduction to *Working Days: The Journals of* The Grapes of Wrath, Robert DeMott reconstructs the monumental effort the novel required of its author. Though Steinbeck wrote *The Grapes of Wrath* in one hundred days between May and October 1938, he had previously spent two years at work on pieces about the Oklahoman migration to California. So trying was this episode in Steinbeck's life, DeMott asserts, that he was never the same afterwards, either as a novelist or as a person. Though critics and the public called for another big social novel, an exhausted Steinbeck immersed himself in other, very different, projects. Robert DeMott has taught American literature at Ohio University and directed San Jose State University's Steinbeck Research Center. He has published several books, including *Steinbeck's Reading*.

I wrote *The Grapes of Wrath* in one hundred days, but many years of preparation preceded it. I take a hell of a long time to get started. The actual writing is the last process.
> —John Steinbeck

John Steinbeck's masterpiece *The Grapes of Wrath* (1939) had a complex foreground and grew through an eventful process of accretion and experimentation. In one way or another, from August 1936, when Steinbeck discovered the plight of the Dust Bowl refugees in California, a subject he told Louis Paul was "like nothing in the world," through October of 1939, when he vowed to put behind him "that part of my life that made the *Grapes*," the "Matter of the Migrants" was Steinbeck's major artistic preoccupation. "The

Reprinted from Robert DeMott, "'Working Days and Hours': Steinbeck's Writing of *The Grapes of Wrath,*" *Modern Fiction Studies*, vol. 18, no. 1, Spring 1990, pp. 3–15, by permission of The Johns Hopkins University Press. Copyright 1990, The Johns Hopkins University Press.

writer can only write about what he admires," Steinbeck claimed, "and since our race admires gallantry, the writer will deal with it where he finds it. He finds it in the struggling poor now." From the moment Steinbeck entered the fray, he prophesied that the presence of the heroic, pioneer-stock Oklahoma migrants would change the fabric of California life. He had little foresight, however, about what his own role in that change would be, how difficult realizing his vision would become, or the degree to which his writing labors would change him.

FOUR STAGES OF THE NOVEL

Between 1936 and 1938 Steinbeck's engagement with his material evolved through at least four major stages of writing: (1) A seven-part series of investigative reports, "The Harvest Gypsies," which appeared October 5–12, 1936, in the San Francisco *News*. (These were reprinted in the spring of 1938 as a pamphlet, *Their Blood Is Strong*, published by the Simon J. Lubin Society with a preface by John Barry.) (2) An unfinished novel, "The Oklahomans," which apparently belonged to late 1937 and which has not survived. (3) A "vicious" 70,000-word anti-vigilante satire, "L'Affaire Lettuceberg," which he finished between February and May of 1938 and then destroyed. And (4) *The Grapes of Wrath*, which was written in one hundred days between late May and late October of 1938.

The ecologically minded Steinbeck wasted little of this material; aspects of setting, conflict, characterization, and theme established in the first three stages found their way into *The Grapes of Wrath*. Each stage shared a fixed core of opposing elements: on one side, the tyranny of California's industrialized agricultural system; on the other side, the innate dignity and resilience of the victimized American migrants. As Steinbeck unequivocally reminded San Francisco *News* columnist John Barry,

> every effort I can bring to bear is and has been at the call of
> the common working people to the end that they may eat
> what they raise, wear what they weave, use what they pro-
> duce, and in every way and in completeness share in the
> works of their hands and their heads. And the reverse is also
> true. I am actively opposed to any man or group who,
> through financial or political control of means of production
> and distribution, is able to control and dominate the lives of
> workers.

KEEPING THE JOURNAL

. . . During the writing of his 200,000-word novel, Steinbeck also kept a journal to record his struggle with the book and with the times from which it emerged. Ninety-nine entries spanning the summer and fall of 1938 constitute the true history of the making of *The Grapes of Wrath.* The entries comprise Steinbeck's attempt "to map the actual working days and hours" of his novel and therefore provide an unparalleled account of the shapings and seizings, the naked slidings, of his creative psyche. Steinbeck's private diary reveals self-doubts, whining, paranoia, and reversals; it also shows dedication, resourcefulness, integrity, and endurance. Taken together, this twin, double-voiced, parallel construction (the public *The Grapes of Wrath* on one side and the private *Working Days* on the other) enacts the process of Steinbeck's humanistic belief and embodies the shape of his artistic faith. . . .

Despite the "leisurely" pace he hoped to establish for his novel, Steinbeck could hardly wait to address the day's fictive project before his concentration waned.

> Now to the day's work and now Muley comes in and the reason for the desertion becomes apparent. Also the night comes with sleeping in the darkening plain and stars. And after that I think a small inter chapter or maybe a large one dealing with the equipment of migration. Well here goes for Muley. Well that is done. I like Muley. He is a fine hater. Must write a few letters now.

Steinbeck's covenant with the fiction-making process took precedence over incendiary sociological or political demands. He was writing a novel, not a journalistic tract. On July 6, just launched into Chapter 13, he stated:

> Now the land work starts again. Now the crossing and I must get into it the feeling of movement and of life. . . . Make the people live. Make them live. But my people must be more than people. They must be an over-essence of people. . . . It is the first day and night. And it has in it the first communication with other migrants. This is important, very important. . . . I simply must get this book done before anything else. No matter what other things are going on. And I can't leave. I must get back to the Joad family on their movement to the west. And now the time has come to go to work. . . . Work is the only good thing.

Maintaining his work intensity was paramount. Without looking back, Steinbeck overcame the disappointing "L'Affaire Lettuceberg," and within a week, or perhaps ten days at the most, he started headlong on the new, unnamed manuscript, which was not actually entitled *The Grapes of Wrath* until early September by Carol Steinbeck, who was typing the novel. However, his work on "L'Affaire" was not wasted because it cleared the way for *The Grapes* by purging his unchecked anger and the desire for his own brand of artistic vengeance. . . .

STEINBECK BEGINS THE NOVEL

The epic scale and technical plan of *Grapes* apparently crystallized between May 15 and May 25 of 1938. During that time, perhaps the most fertile germinative moment in Steinbeck's writing life, the organizational form of the novel, with its alternating chapters of exposition and narrative, leaped to life in his mind. Steinbeck was not an elite literary practitioner, but he achieved in *The Grapes of Wrath* a compelling combination of individual style, visual realism, and rambunctious, symphonic form that was at once accessible and experimental, documentarian and fictive, expository and lyrical. He envisioned the novel whole, all the way down to the subversive last scene "ready for so long" (Rose of Sharon giving her breast to a starving man), which became both the propelling image of the book and the imaginative climax toward which the entire novel moved.

Indeed, except for a few afterthoughts and insertions, *The Grapes of Wrath* was written with remarkably pre-ordained motion and directed passion. Steinbeck apparently did not work from a formal outline (nothing of the kind has ever turned up); rather, he sketched out the novel in his head in aggregate first, followed by a brief planning session each day. While Steinbeck vacillated about his ability to execute the plan, he showed few reservations about the plan itself. On June 10 he wrote in his work diary:

> With luck I should be finished with this first draft in October sometime and then God knows what I'll do. I'll surely be ready for a rest. Sometimes now I get a little bit tired just with the multitude of this story but the movement is so fascinating that I don't stay tired. And the leisurely pace is good too. This must be a good book. It simply must. I haven't any choice. It must be far and away the best thing I've ever attempted—slow but sure, piling detail on detail until a picture and an experience emerge. Until the whole throbbing thing emerges. And I can do it. I feel very strong to do it. Today for instance into the picture is the evening and the cooking of the rabbits and

the discussion of prison and punishment. And the owls and the cat catches a mouse and they sit on the sloping porch. And tomorrow the beginning of the used car yard if I am finished with this scene. Better make this scene three pages instead of two. Because there can never be too much of background. Well to work on the characters. Friday's work is done and I think pretty good work.

From the outset Steinbeck possessed an intuitive sense of rightness concerning the direction his book and his characters would take. Indeed, *The Grapes of Wrath* embodies the form of his attention: in the entire handwritten manuscript of 165 12" x 18" ledger pages, the number of deletions and emendations are so few and infrequent as to be nearly nonexistent. Despite his late stretch-drive doubts, and the refrain of self-deprecation that sounds throughout the work diary, the truth is that in writing *The Grapes of Wrath* Steinbeck was creating with the full potency of his imaginative powers. His ability to execute a work of its reach and magnitude so flawlessly places him among the premier creative talents of his age. From the vantage point of history, the venture stands as one of those happy occasions when a writer simply wrote better than he thought he could.

Steinbeck set out immediately to establish a unified work rhythm, a "single track mind" that would allow him to complete the enormous task in approximately five months. Though he had written steadily throughout the 1930s (he published eleven books and limited editions in the first eight years of the decade), the work never seemed to get easier. Averaging 2000 words a day (some days as few as 800, some days, when the juices were flowing, as many as 2200), Steinbeck began the novel unhurriedly to keep its "tempo" under control, hoping at the same time to keep alive the large rhythmic structure of the novel. . . .

COMPLICATIONS IN WRITING AND LIFE

Steinbeck's anxiety escalated during the late summer, his pace became increasingly frenetic, and his work became a chore. That he completed the novel within the time he had allotted testifies to his discipline, resilience, will power, and singleness of purpose. His story of making his novel is a dramatic testimony to triumph over intrusions, obstacles, and self-inflicted doubts. Nearly each day brought unsolicited requests for his name and new demands on his time, including unscheduled visitors, unanticipated disruptions, and reversals. . . .

Emerging ahead of his accomplishments seemed to Steinbeck insurmountable at times that summer, because major interruptions kept occurring, any one of which might have sidetracked a less dedicated writer. August proved the most embattled time of all. Early in the month Steinbeck noted in his journal: "There are now four things or five rather to write through—throat, bankruptcy, Pare [filmmaker Pare Lorentz], ranch, and the book." His litany of woes included Carol's painful tonsil operation, which temporarily incapacitated her; the bankruptcy of Steinbeck's publisher, Covici-Friede, which threatened the end of steady royalty payments and an uncertain publishing future for the novel he was writing; Pare Lorentz's offer to involve Steinbeck in making a film version of *In Dubious Battle*; the purchase of the Biddle Ranch, which Carol wanted badly and Steinbeck felt compelled to buy for her (they argued over the pressure this caused); and the book itself, still untitled (and therefore still without "being"), which now seemed more recalcitrant than ever. Except for the making of the film, all these dilemmas resolved themselves, though not always quickly enough for Steinbeck. On August 16, in the middle of what he called a "Bad, Lazy Time," he lamented:

> Demoralization complete and seemingly unbeatable. So many things happening that I can't not be interested. . . . All this is more excitement than our whole lives put together. All crowded into a month. . . . My many weaknesses are beginning to show their heads. I simply must get this thing out of my system. I'm not a writer. I've been fooling myself and other people. I wish I were. This success will ruin me as sure as hell. It probably won't last, and that will be all right. I'll try to go on with work now. Just a stint every day does it, I keep forgetting.

Although Steinbeck did not believe writing was a team sport, the fact is *The Grapes of Wrath* profited from the involvement of other people, primarily [government camp manager] Tom Collins, who kept Steinbeck supplied with much of the basic field information he needed to make his novel accurate and detailed, and Carol Steinbeck, who besides typing the novel, served her husband in most other imaginable capacities. By dedicating the novel to them, Steinbeck properly acknowledged their contributions. . . .

THE FINAL DRIVE

In early October, rebuked often enough by his wife's example and by her words (Ma Joad's indomitableness owes much to Carol's spirit), Steinbeck roused himself from "self-indulgence" and "laziness" to mount the final drive. The last five chapters of the novel came to him so abundantly that he had more material than he could use. A few days from the end Steinbeck was so tired he nearly collapsed. He was again assailed with "grave doubts" about his "run-of-the-mill" book. And then, in one of those magical transferences artists are heir to in moments of extreme exhaustion or receptivity, Steinbeck believed that Tom Joad, his fictive alter ego, not only floated above the novel's "last pages . . . like a spirit," but he imagined that Joad actually entered the novelist's work space, the private chamber of his soul: "Tom! Tom! Tom!" Steinbeck wrote on October 20. "I know. It wasn't him. Yes, I think I can go on now. In fact, I feel stronger. Much stronger. Funny where the energy comes from. Now to work, only now it isn't work anymore." With that visitation, that benediction, Steinbeck arrived at the intersection of novel and journal, a luminous point where the life of the writer and the creator of life merge. The terms of the complex investment fulfilled, Steinbeck needed only three more days to complete *The Grapes of Wrath.*

Finally, sometime around noon on Wednesday, October 26, Steinbeck, "so dizzy" he could "hardly see the page," completed the last 775 words of the novel: "Finished this day—and I hope to God it's good." At the bottom of the concluding manuscript page, Steinbeck, whose writing was normally minuscule, scrawled in letters an inch-and-a-half high, "END#." It should have been cause for joyous celebration, but between bouts of bone-weary tiredness and nervous exhaustion, he felt only numbness and maybe a little of the mysterious satisfaction that comes from having given his all. . . .

A CHANGED MAN

Steinbeck did not quit writing as he once threatened to do, but by the early 1940s, no longer content to be the chronicler of Depression-era subjects, he went afield to find new roots, new sources, new forms. Between 1940 and 1943, for example, Steinbeck's artistic quest resulted in unpublished poetry (a suite of twenty-five love poems for Gwyn [Conger, a young actress with whom he had begun an affair]), an unfinished satire ("The God in the Pipes"), and a completed novel written in first-person point of view, which was an unprecedented technical choice for Steinbeck (*Lifeboat;* only marginally the basis for Hitchcock's 1944 film). His restless "ranges and searches" also led to one of his most important publications, the collaborative travel and marine biology book, *Sea of Cortez: A Leisurely Journal of Travel and Research* (with Edward F. Ricketts). During this period he also wrote a documentary film script, *The Forgotten Village;* a play-novel, *The Moon Is Down;* a patriotic documentary book, *Bombs Away: The Story of a Bomber Team;* and war journalism for the New York *Herald-Tribune* (later collected as *Once There Was a War*). Clearly, he had energy to spare, though it no longer went into epic structures like *The Grapes of Wrath* but into the "foundation of some new discipline. . . ."

Many "have speculated," his biographer writes, "about what happened to change Steinbeck after *The Grapes of Wrath*. One answer is that what happened was the writing of the novel itself." Here, surely, is a private tragedy, a cautionary tale, to parallel the tragic aspects of his fiction: an isolated individual writer composed a novel that extolled a social group's capacity for survival in a hostile economic world but was himself so nearly tractored under in the process that the unique qualities (the angle of vision, the vital signature, the moral indignation) that made his art exemplary in the first place could never be repeated with the same integrated force. If *The Grapes of Wrath* permanently changed the literary landscape of American fiction and altered the public's awareness about the socioeconomic nightmare caused by the Dust Bowl, the Depression, and the corporate farm industry, the book also changed Steinbeck permanently. In his journal Steinbeck had the prescience to commit to words the inside narrative of his most focused years. Laboring over *The Grapes of Wrath* meant Steinbeck would never be the same writer again. His change from 1930s social realist to 1940s experimentalist was not caused by a bankruptcy of talent or even a failure of nerve. Rather, it was the backlash of an unprecedented success, a repugnant "posterity," that turned Steinbeck so painfully self-conscious, and so deeply disgusted with the imposed limits of proletarian subject matter and form, he could never again return to the "Matter of the Migrants," even though his critical audience clamored for him to do so, and turned hostile when he refused.

The Title of the Novel

Jackson J. Benson

In this excerpt from his massive biography, *The True Adventures of John Steinbeck*, published in 1984, Jackson J. Benson relates how Steinbeck's first wife, Carol, came up with the title *The Grapes of Wrath*. Steinbeck believed that this title would give the novel the precise focus that he wanted: it suggested a new, social revolution while undercutting accusations that his book was anti-American. At Steinbeck's insistence his publisher printed the complete lyrics of "The Battle Hymn of the Republic," from which the title is taken, on the novel's endpapers. Jackson J. Benson has taught at San Diego State University and is the author of books on Ernest Hemingway and Wallace Stegner.

At the beginning of September [1938] Carol [Steinbeck] had come up with a brilliant idea for the title of the new book: the title, "The Grapes of Wrath," gave the book a dynamic focus, and the words of the hymn it referred to could be applied in numerous ways to the novel's contents. John was delighted, and he wrote to both [publishers] Covici and Otis to ask them how they liked it. A week later he wrote to Otis:

> About the title—Pat wired that he liked it. And I am glad because I too like it better all the time. I think it is Carol's best title so far. I like it because it is a march and this book is a kind of march—because it is in our own revolutionary tradition and because in reference to this book it has a large meaning. And I like it because people know the Battle Hymn who don't know the Star Spangled Banner.

He particularly liked the title because it gave an American stamp to his material. From previous experience he knew that there would be those who would try to smear the book as foreign-inspired, and he wanted to blunt such an attack from the outset because he felt very strongly that what he was describing was an American phenomenon. For several

Excerpted from "Poverty and Success," from *The True Adventures of John Steinbeck, Writer*, by Jackson J. Benson. Copyright © 1984 by Jackson J. Benson. Used by permission of Viking Penguin, a division of Penguin Putnam Inc.

years, . . . Steinbeck had expressed the belief that the country was undergoing a kind of revolution. Although he appears to have been vague in his own mind as to what form the conflict would eventually take or what would be its ultimate results, he saw the movement as a phalanx of little people in our society, workers and small farmers, too proud and independent to be pushed around indefinitely by those who had grabbed a disproportionate amount of the country's wealth and power.

WRITING ABOUT CLASS

After the publication of *The Grapes of Wrath*, Steinbeck wrote a radio interview script (never aired) in which he provided both questions and answers, the major subject of which was this movement in American society as the theme of the novel. In response to the question, "In the growing American literature there was no such cleavage between so-called classes as seems to be at the core of present day writing. Can you account for this?" Steinbeck answered, in part:

> Before the country was settled, the whole drive of the country by both rich and poor was to settle it. To this end they worked together. The menaces were Indians, weather, loneliness and the quality of the unknown. But this phase ended. When there was no longer unlimited land for everyone, then battles developed for what there was. And then as always, those few who had financial resources and financial brains had little difficulty in acquiring the land in larger and larger blocks. . . . This condition left the great people in their original desire for the security symbol land but this time the menace (as they say in Hollywood) had changed. It was no longer Indians and weather and loneliness, it had become the holders of the land. . . . Now, since the people go on with their struggle, the writer still sets down that struggle and still sets down the opponents. The opponents or rather the obstacle to the desired end right now happens to be those individuals and groups of financiers who by the principle of ownership withhold security from the mass of the people. And since this is so, this is the material the writer deals in.

Later he describes this struggle in biological terms:

> The human like any other life form will tolerate an unhealthful condition for some time, and then will either die or will overcome the condition either by mutation or by destroying the unhealthful condition. Since there seems little tendency for the human race to become extinct, and since one cannot through biological mutation overcome the necessity for eating, I judge that the final method will be the one chosen.

"THE BATTLE HYMN OF THE REPUBLIC"

Steinbeck told his publisher, Pascal Covici, to include "all, all, all" of the lyrics to "The Battle Hymn of the Republic" in the novel, and Covici obliged. The lyrics, written by Julia Ward Howe during the Civil War (the tune was in existence long before), were an inspiration to the Union army.

Mine eyes have seen the glory of the coming of the Lord:
He is trampling out the vintage where the grapes of wrath are
stored;
He hath loosed the fateful lightning of His terrible swift
sword;
          His truth is marching on.

CHORUS
Glory, glory, hallelujah!
Glory, glory, hallelujah!
Glory, glory, hallelujah!
His truth is marching on.

I have seen Him in the watch-fires of a hundred circling
camps,
They have builded Him an altar in the evening dews and
damps;
I have read His righteous sentence by the dim and flaring
lamps;
          His day is marching on.

I have read His fiery gospel writ in rows of burnished steel!
"As ye deal with My contemners, so with you My grace shall
deal!
Let the Hero, born of woman, crush the serpent with His
heel,"
          Since God is marching on.

He has sounded forth the trumpet that shall never call retreat;
He is searching out the hearts of men before His judgment
seat,
O be swift, my soul, to answer Him! be jubilant, my feet!
          Our God is marching on.

In the beauty of the lilies Christ was born across the sea,
With a glory in His bosom that transfigures you and me;
As He died to make men holy, let us die to make men free,
          While God is marching on.

C.A. Browne, *The Story of Our National Ballads.* New York: Thomas Y. Crowell, 1960.

A NEW AMERICAN REVOLUTION

He saw the Okie migration as a smaller phalanx within the larger, and he also notes in his "interview" that in writing *The Grapes of Wrath*, "I have set down what a large section of our people are doing and wanting, and symbolically what all people of all time are doing and wanting. This migration is the outward sign of the want." It was a movement, both literally and figuratively, that for the purpose of this novel could be used as a metaphor for the social revolution as a whole. And just as the larger movement had, in his mind, its antecedents in the American Revolution, so too the Dust Bowl phalanx had its earlier parallel in the movement west of the settlers. In an interview with the *San Jose Mercury* during the composition of *The Grapes of Wrath*, he said, referring to the Okies: "Their coming here now is going to change things almost as much as did the coming of the first American settlers. . . . These people have the same vitality . . . and they know just what they want."

AN AMERICAN BOOK

Knowing the American small farmer and worker better than either the capitalists or the communists, he was certain that the conflict, whatever forms it might take, would be made on our own terms, in terms of the "Battle Hymn of the Republic," rather than the "Internationale" [the anthem of the Russian Revolution]. And to underscore the point, he decided he would like to have the hymn, words and music, printed on the endpapers at the front and back of the book. When the idea came to him, he sent a wire to Covici, and followed up the request several times in letters. He was insistent, knowing that publishers do not take very seriously authorial suggestions regarding format. He wrote Covici in January:

> The fascist crowd will try to sabotage this book because it is revolutionary. They will try to give it the communist angle. However, the Battle Hymn is American and intensely so. Further, every American child learns it and then forgets the words. So if both words and music are there the book is keyed into the American scene from the beginning.

When he got the proofs in February, Covici had given in to the extent of printing the first verse as a sort of prologue quotation to the novel. Steinbeck wrote, "I mean Pat to print *all all all* the verses of the Battle Hymn. They're all pertinent and they're all exciting. And the music if you can." Covici obliged.

The Real Migrants

John Steinbeck

In 1936 Steinbeck covered the plight of migrant farmers in California for the *San Francisco News*. His investigative reports ran under the title *The Harvest Gypsies* and were later collected and published as *Their Blood Is Strong*. In this excerpt Steinbeck documents the terrible conditions that existed among the migrants. The illness, malnutrition, and misfortune he describes prefigure the Joads' calamities in California. In particular, Steinbeck's account of the conditions under which migrant women delivered their babies without medical care is reminiscent of the scene late in *The Grapes of Wrath* in which Rose of Sharon delivers a stillborn infant.

Migrant families in California find that unemployment relief, which is available to settled unemployed, has little to offer them. In the first place there has grown up a regular technique for getting relief; one who knows the ropes can find aid from the various state and Federal disbursement agencies, while a man ignorant of the methods will be turned away.

The migrant is always partially unemployed. The nature of his occupation makes his work seasonal. At the same time the nature of his work makes him ineligible for relief. The basis for receiving most of the relief is residence.

But it is impossible for the migrant to accomplish the residence. He must move about the country. He could not stop long enough to establish residence or he would starve to death. He finds, then, on application, that he cannot be put on the relief rolls. And being ignorant, he gives up at that point.

For the same reason he finds that he cannot receive any of the local benefits reserved for residents of a county. The county hospital was built not for the transient, but for residents of the county.

Reprinted from "The Harvest Gypsies," by John Steinbeck, in *"The Grapes of Wrath" and Other Writings, 1936–1941* (New York: Library of America, 1996). Copyright 1936 San Francisco News. Reprinted by permission of McIntosh and Otis, Inc.

THE HISTORY OF ONE MIGRANT FAMILY

It will be interesting to trace the history of one family in relation to medicine, work relief and direct relief. The family consisted of five persons, a man of 50, his wife of 45, two boys, 15 and 12, and a girl of six. They came from Oklahoma, where the father operated a little ranch of 50 acres of prairie.

When the ranch dried up and blew away the family put its moveable possessions in an old Dodge truck and came to California. They arrived in time for the orange picking in Southern California and put in a good average season.

The older boy and the father together made $60. At that time the automobile broke out some teeth of the differential and the repairs, together with three second-hand tires, took $22. The family moved into Kern County to chop grapes and camped in the squatters' camp on the edge of Bakersfield.

PROBLEMS BEGIN

At this time the father sprained his ankle and the little girl developed measles. Doctors' bills amounted to $10 of the remaining store, and food and transportation took most of the rest.

The 15-year-old boy was now the only earner for the family. The 12-year-old boy picked up a brass gear in a yard and took it to sell.

He was arrested and taken before the juvenile court, but was released to his father's custody. The father walked in to Bakersfield from the squatters' camp on a sprained ankle because the gasoline was gone from the automobile and he didn't dare invest any of the remaining money in more gasoline.

This walk caused complications in the sprain which laid him up again. The little girl had recovered from measles by this time, but her eyes had not been protected and she had lost part of her eyesight.

The father now applied for relief and found that he was ineligible because he had not established the necessary residence. All resources were gone. A little food was given to the family by neighbors in the squatters' camp.

A neighbor who had a goat brought in a cup of milk every day for the little girl.

TRAGEDY ENSUES

At this time the 15-year-old boy came home from the fields with a pain in his side. He was feverish and in great pain.

The mother put hot cloths on his stomach while a neighbor took the crippled father to the county hospital to apply for aid. The hospital was full, all its time taken by bona fide local residents. The trouble described as a pain in the stomach by the father was not taken seriously.

The father was given a big dose of salts to take home to the boy. That night the pain grew so great that the boy became unconscious. The father telephoned the hospital and found that there was no one on duty who could attend to his case. The boy died of a burst appendix the next day.

There was no money. The county buried him free. The father sold the Dodge for $30 and bought a $2 wreath for the funeral. With the remaining money he laid in a store of cheap, filling food—beans, oatmeal, lard. He tried to go back to work in the fields. Some of the neighbors gave him rides to work and charged him a small amount for transportation.

He was on the weak ankle too soon and could not make over 75¢ a day at piece-work, chopping. Again he applied for relief and was refused because he was not a resident and because he was employed. The little girl, because of insufficient food and weakness from measles, relapsed into influenza.

The father did not try the county hospital again. He went to a private doctor who refused to come to the squatters' camp unless he were paid in advance. The father took two days' pay and gave it to the doctor who came to the family shelter, took the girl's temperature, gave the mother seven pills, told the mother to keep the child warm and went away. The father lost his job because he was too slow.

He applied again for help and was given one week's supply of groceries.

ONE IN THOUSANDS

This can go on indefinitely. The case histories like it can be found in their thousands. It may be argued that there were ways for this man to get aid, but how did he know where to get it? There was no way for him to find out.

California communities have used the old, old methods of dealing with such problems. The first method is to disbelieve it and vigorously to deny that there is a problem. The second is to deny local responsibility since the people are not permanent residents. And the third and silliest of all is to run the trouble over the county borders into another county. The floater method of swapping what the counties consider unde-sirables from hand to hand is like a game of medicine ball.

A fine example of this insular stupidity concerns the hookworm situation in Stanislaus County. The mud along water courses where there are squatters living is infected. Several businessmen of Modesto and Ceres offered as a so-lution that the squatters be cleared out. There was no thought of isolating the victims and stopping the hookworm.

The affected people were, according to these men, to be run out of the county to spread the disease in other fields. It is this refusal of the counties to consider anything but the immediate economy and profit of the locality that is the cause of a great deal of the unsolvable quality of the migrants' problem. The counties seem terrified that they may be required to give some aid to the labor they require for their harvests.

According to several Government and state surveys and studies of large numbers of migrants, the maximum a worker can make is $400 a year, while the average is around $300, and the large minimum is $150 a year. This amount must feed, clothe and transport whole families.

A POOR DIET

Sometimes whole families are able to work in the fields, thus making an additional wage. In other observed cases a whole family, weakened by sickness and malnutrition, has worked in the fields, making less than the wage of one healthy man. It does not take long at the migrants' work to reduce the health of any family. Food is scarce always, and luxuries of any kind are unknown.

Observed diets run something like this when the family is making money:

Family of eight—Boiled cabbage, baked sweet potatoes, creamed carrots, beans, fried dough, jelly, tea.

Family of seven—Beans, baking-powder biscuits, jam, coffee.

Family of six—Canned salmon, cornbread, raw onions.

Family of five—Biscuits, fried potatoes, dandelion greens, pears.

These are dinners. It is to be noticed that even in these flush times there is no milk, no butter. The major part of the diet is starch. In slack times the diet becomes all starch, this being the cheapest way to fill up. Dinners during lay-offs are as follows:

Family of seven—Beans, fried dough.

Family of six—Fried cornmeal.

Family of five—Oatmeal mush.

Family of eight (there were six children)—Dandelion greens and boiled potatoes.

It will be seen that even in flush times the possibility of remaining healthy is very slight. The complete absence of milk for the children is responsible for many of the diseases of malnutrition. Even pellagra is far from unknown.

The preparation of food is the most primitive. Cooking equipment usually consists of a hole dug in the ground or a kerosene can with a smoke vent and open front.

If the adults have been working 10 hours in the fields or in the packing sheds they do not want to cook. They will buy canned goods as long as they have money, and when they are low in funds they will subsist on half-cooked starches.

CHILDBIRTH

The problem of childbirth among the migrants is among the most terrible. There is no prenatal care of the mothers whatever, and no possibility of such care. They must work in the fields until they are physically unable or, if they do not work, the care of the other children and of the camp will not allow the prospective mothers any rest.

In actual birth the presence of a doctor is a rare exception. Sometimes in the squatters' camps a neighbor woman will help at the birth. There will be no sanitary precautions nor hygienic arrangements. The child will be born on newspapers in the dirty bed. In case of a bad presentation requiring surgery or forceps, the mother is practically condemned to death. Once born, the eyes of the baby are not treated, the endless medical attention lavished on middle-class babies is completely absent.

The mother, usually suffering from malnutrition, is not able to produce breast milk. Sometimes the baby is nourished on canned milk until it can eat fried dough and cornmeal. This being the case, the infant mortality is very great.

A SUCCESSION OF DEAD CHILDREN

The following is an example: Wife of family with three children. She is 38; her face is lined and thin and there is a hard glaze on her eyes. The three children who survive were born prior to 1929, when the family rented a farm in Utah. In 1930 this woman bore a child which lived four months and died of "colic."

In 1931 her child was born dead because "a han' truck fulla boxes run inta me two days before the baby come." In 1932 there was a miscarriage. "I couldn't carry the baby 'cause I was sick." She is ashamed of this. In 1933 her baby lived a week. "Jus' died. I don't know what of." In 1934 she had no pregnancy. She is also a little ashamed of this. In 1935 her baby lived a long time, nine months.

"Seemed for a long time like he was gonna live. Big strong fella it seemed like." She is pregnant again now. "If we could get milk for um I guess it'd be better." This is an extreme case, but by no means an unusual one.

Other Possible Endings for *The Grapes of Wrath*

Jules Chametzky

Jules Chametzky tackles the issue of the ending of
The Grapes of Wrath, which caused controversy even
before the novel was published. Chametzky argues
that Steinbeck could have chosen one of two alternative endings for the novel, at the government camp at
Weedpatch or during the flood as a group of men attempt to build a dike to hold off the rising waters.
But Steinbeck rejects both these endings, Chametzky
suggests, due to his distrust of organization and his
belief in the value of the individual: The Weedpatch
ending is too suggestive of big government as savior,
while the dike scene's "proletarian" quality has
Marxist implications that Steinbeck wanted to avoid.
Chametzky concludes that Steinbeck's ending is the
appropriate one for the novel. Jules Chametzky has
taught at the University of Massachusetts. He is the
author of a number of books on American culture.

A few years ago Theodore Pollack called attention once
again to the conclusion of *The Grapes of Wrath*, arguing that
far from being an example of "rank sentimentalism" or
"overdone . . . symbolism," the ending "successfully and art-
fully" concluded the important theme of reproduction that
threads its way through the book. His case rests, finally, on
the observation that the book begins in "drought and despair," but concludes in a gigantic rainstorm and a kind of
rebirth, which suggests the end of "the curse of sterility," for
now all is "water and hope." I find this an interesting, but
somewhat dubious interpretation, since the storm at the end
may as easily—and more convincingly—be seen as just one
more tribulation heaped upon the Joads; yet the effort to integrate the ending with the rest of the novel is admirable and

Reprinted from Jules Chametzky, "The Ambivalent Endings of *The Grapes of Wrath*,"
Modern Fiction Studies, vol. 11, no. 1, Spring 1965, pp. 35–44, by permission of The
Johns Hopkins University Press. Copyright 1965 by The Johns Hopkins University
Press.

wholly understandable. For there is a stubborn sense in which it is the right ending; at the same time, there is also a sense in which it fails to fulfill certain expectations aroused in the book. . . .

My chief assumption is that there are in the book two other points at which Steinbeck could have concluded his saga of the Joad family, his inventory of wrongs done them, and the measures necessary to relieve those wrongs. That there are three possible endings discernible—and reasons why two were rejected in favor of a third—suggests a tension among various impulses, intentions, and values in the novel that Steinbeck may not have satisfactorily resolved.

The book ends, as we all remember, with a startling, vivid scene. At the end of the novel, the Joads seem to have reached the lowest point of their lives: jobless, homeless, fleeing from the rains and flood that have destroyed their temporary refuge in a deserted box-car, they make their way to a deserted barn on higher ground. There they encounter two other homeless people—a boy and his sick father. The father is starving to death and must have nourishment to revive him. Rose of Sharon, whose baby has been stillborn, still has her breasts full of milk. She and Ma Joad exchange deep looks, Rose of Sharon says simply "Yes," and the book ends as she lies down by the dying man, presenting him her life-giving milk as she smiles "mysteriously."

From the first, this ending has been an object of attention by the critics. Clifton Fadiman thought "this ending [was] the tawdriest kind of fake symbolism"; Bernard De Voto thought it was "symbolism gone sentimental"; Edward Berry Burgum thought it "meretricious" and only a symbolic gesture, unprepared for in the novel; Claude-Edmonde Magny argued that it was "a purely poetic image which in no way brings the plot to a conclusion." These criticisms, and others like them, share the assumption that the reader is somehow cheated by the ending. Steinbeck seems to have aroused certain expectations in the novel that remain unfulfilled. . . .

A POSSIBLE ENDING AT WEEDPATCH

The book *could* have ended with the picture of life in Weedpatch, the government camp. This would have provided what I will call "The New Deal" ending, familiar enough in the literature of the period and in such classic documentary films of the thirties as Pare Lorentz's "The River" and "The

City." The pattern of these works inspired by the New Deal is simply to contrast the waste and destruction of human or natural resources that result from an anarchic and un-planned set of conditions with the order, harmony, and con-structive dignity to be achieved through cooperation, plan-ning and a rational disposition of resources used for the common good.

This is precisely the contrast revealed in the Joads' expe-rience in Weedpatch. The savagery and horror of life outside the camp—the world of an unprincipled, frightened free en-terprise system—is opposed to the well-ordered government camp, which is depicted as a model of what could be achieved as regards cleanliness, health, pleasure, and the renewed dignity of a depressed and exploited people. In working together with others in this context, the Joads' sus-picious individuality, Ma's "meanness" and "shame," forced upon them "out there," is broken down and replaced with an enduring sense of the value of participation in cooperative, even communal, units larger than the family. . . .

WEEDPATCH REJECTED

If this form of organization is so good, why then does Stein-beck shrink back from the implications of Tom Joad's "Well, for Christ's sake! Why ain't they more places like this?" It is not enough to say that there was no remunerative work to be found, so that ultimately the Joads had to leave the haven of the government camp. The logic of the situation clearly sug-gests an obvious solution: let the government supply work. In rejecting this as the climactic moment in the novel, Stein-beck lets the suggestion stanch, but only as a suggestion, not hardening it into something more programmatic. The inter-esting point is not that Steinbeck seems to recoil from a rev-olutionary position—or that, as Mr. [Warren] French affirms, "Steinbeck is definitely no collectivist"—but rather that he both advances towards and retreats from such an idea. It is worth investigating. How is it that the question of his being a collectivist comes up at all, only to be denied?

Of course, from an esthetic point of view, Steinbeck's re-jection of the government camp as his climax is sheer gain. For if Steinbeck had stopped on this happily "up-beat" note most of us would feel, I suspect, justifiably cheated. It would have failed because of its very neatness and its conformity to the prevalent didactic formula I have called "New Deal." By

STEINBECK DEFENDS HIS ENDING

In this letter to his publisher, Pascal "Pat" Covici, Steinbeck explains why he will not change the ending to The Grapes of Wrath, *despite Covici's request.*

Los Gatos
January 16, 1939

Dear Pat:

I have your letter today. And I am sorry but I cannot change that ending. It is casual—there is no fruity climax, it is not more important than any other part of the book—if there is a symbol, it is a survival symbol not a love symbol, it must be an accident, it must be a stranger, and it must be quick. To build this stranger into the structure of the book would be to warp the whole meaning of the book. The fact that the Joads don't know him, don't care about him, have no ties to him— that is the emphasis. The giving of the breast has no more sentiment than the giving of a piece of bread. I'm sorry if that doesn't get over. It will maybe. I've been on this design and balance for a long time and I think I know how I want it. And if I'm wrong, I'm alone in my wrongness. . . .

The incident of the earth mother feeding by the breast is older than literature. You know that I have never been touchy about changes, but I have too many thousands of hours on this book, every incident has been too carefully chosen and its weight judged and fitted. The balance is there. One other thing—I am not writing a satisfying story. I've done my damndest to rip a reader's nerves to rags, I don't want him satisfied.

And still one more thing—I tried to write this book the way lives are being lived not the way books are written.

This letter sounds angry. I don't mean it to be. I know that books lead to a strong deep climax. This one doesn't except by implication and the reader must bring the implication to it. If he doesn't, it wasn't a book for him to read. Throughout I've tried to make the reader participate in the actuality, what he takes from it will be scaled entirely on his own depth or hollowness. There are five layers in this book, a reader will find as many as he can and he won't find more than he has in himself.

Elaine Steinbeck and Robert Wallsten, eds., *Steinbeck: A Life in Letters.* New York: Penguin, 1975.

following such a formula, Steinbeck would have abandoned a chief function of serious literature, which is to do justice to a complex rather than a black-and-white or programmatic version of reality. But there is another, an ideological, reason for Steinbeck's refusal to do more than suggest the revolutionary implications—not the reformist ones—behind Tom Joad's question.

Steinbeck was unable to resolve satisfactorily his awareness that only through organization, of greater or lesser complexity, can the problems—of greater or lesser complexity—of modern society and of the individual within it be settled ("This here camp is a organization," says one of the Okies proudly, which can solve for them the problem of self-defense and more), with his equally deep distrust of both organization and the modern society that demands it. This distrust can easily be shown in Steinbeck's attitude towards technology—or, to put it more simply, the machine—which is, after all, possible only as the result of complex, highly organized forms of behavior and is indeed a perfect expression of it. Steinbeck's attitude is, at best, ambivalent. . . .

Steinbeck was committed in part, at least, to an agrarian vision of a society of small, independent land-holders, which is Tom Joad's final vision, too ("all farm our own land"). In such a society a natural, almost pastorally simple relation of man to the soil could presumably be maintained, and such a vision and commitment go deeper in Steinbeck—is certainly more emotionally charged, as the lines above show—than any commitment to reform based on the idea of a planned economy. This image of felicity is threatened with destruction by the realities of modern society which, like the machine that is its perfect expression, is powerful, inhuman, and threatens the very existence of humanity. The turtle depicted in Chapter Three, like mankind slowly making its way across the road, is hit by a machine—a truck. Such is the threat, deeply felt by Steinbeck. The turtle survives, however, and even adds to the continuation of life: "as the turtle crawled on down the embankment, its shell dragged dirt over the seeds." Ma Joad says toward the end of the book: "People is goin' on—changin' a little, maybe, but goin' right on." These sentiments I take to be an expression of Steinbeck's faith, not of his ideology, which remains fixed in the contradiction between the good *and* the horrors that can flow from complex, highly organized forms of life. Could we have the good that might come from "more government camps" without the horrors of a vast, machine-like, highly organized, "unnatural" way of life that such a program might suggest? Some such awareness must lie behind Steinbeck's advance and retreat from this solution—to his book and to the problem of establishing the Joads' shattered individuality within a larger framework of allegiances.

These same considerations underlie the advance towards and retreat from the second ending. Leaving Weedpatch, the Joads become, unwittingly, strikebreakers on a fruit ranch. His curiosity piqued by the armed-camp atmosphere of the place, Tom Joad makes contact with the strikers outside the gate. He discovers that the leader is an old friend, a former preacher named Jim Casy, and witnesses his brutal murder by a deputy sheriff. Enraged, Tom kills the deputy, is himself wounded, and must become a fugitive. But his experiences, especially the effect of Jim Casy's life and death, have completed his education. He says to Ma Joad, just before he leaves for good, "But I know now a fella ain't no good alone," and "an' I been wonderin' if all our folks got together an' yelled," and "I'll be ever'where—wherever you look. Wherever they's a fight so hungry people can eat, I'll be there. Wherever they's a cop beatin' up a guy, I'll be there. If Casy knowed, why, I'll be in the way guys yell when they're mad an'—I'll be in the way kids laugh when they're hungry an' they know supper's ready. An' when our folks eat the stuff they raise an' live in the houses they build—why, I'll be there. See? God, I'm talkin' like Casy."

A short while later, the Joads have taken refuge from heavy rains in a deserted box-car. Rosasharn begins to have labor pains just as flood threatens this improvised home. In order to gain time for the birth of the baby, the men must organize themselves and build a dike against the flood. For a while their strenuous efforts prevail: "She'd come over if we hadn' a built up," Pa Joad cries triumphantly. At this point, we have reached a conceivable ending of the novel. If the government camp derives from a New Deal convention, in these scenes of Tom's leaving and the struggle against the flood (with its obvious symbolic portentousness) we are in the presence of certain conventions deriving from proletarian fiction—so allow me to call this Steinbeck's "proletarian" ending to *The Grapes of Wrath.*

A few words must be said about the "proletarian fiction" which flourished rather sporadically between the years 1930 and 1935, and which Steinbeck freshly and originally explored in *In Dubious Battle.* In theory, no one was precisely sure what the form of this genre was, but in practice during those years a spate of novels and stories—mostly stillborn because of their doctrinaire origin and intention—were written centering on the conditions of working-class life. The dramatic action often favored as a unifying or climactic device was a strike, since a strike was presumably the most aggravated and dramatic expression of class-warfare. Within a more or less patterned framework, the depiction of a strike was eminently suitable for driving home certain lessons dear to the hearts of the idealogues sponsoring or writing such fiction: the need for workers' solidarity behind a trained, class-conscious leadership, and the perfidies of the bourgeoisie. The setting was often a small town, so that all the connections between bosses, police, courts and other institutions of the bourgeoisie could be more easily traced. There was usually a worker, naive at the outset, who developed class-consciousness and militancy through struggle, often after a martyrdom of one or more workers. Finally, the strike was invariably crushed by the powerful forces aligned against the workers, although the new worker, forged in steel, would go on to carry the battle along.

It will be seen that Tom Joad fits nicely into the pattern. He could qualify as the naive worker who learns through hard-knocks—usually involving the martyrdom of another worker (Jim Casy's last words to those killing him, "You don' know what you're a-doin'," echo Christ's last words)—and then goes on, stronger and more "aware," to continue the fight. However, the tableau at the dike could easily be made to represent the workers' education in action to a knowledge of their own strength in solidarity, which could be the occasion for the birth of a new life on the ruins of the old. None of this contradicts, *essentially*, the central theme of Steinbeck's novel, the education of the Joads. Why then does Steinbeck reject it—the dike breaks, the child is stillborn—and move on towards his final resolution?

REJECTION OF THE PROLETARIAN ENDING

In my crude and perhaps over-simplifying view, the reason has to do with certain postulates of Marxianism [philosophy based on the works of Karl Marx] that is the basis of much "proletarian" writing. While suggesting a logical, even "positive," ending to the book, Marxism as a system of thought and a way of regarding the world would, in its extreme rationalism, reject Steinbeck's almost mystical reverence for an unspoiled man-earth relationship as well as his antimachine animus. There would therefore have to be a deep resistance in him towards such a system of thought. Advocates of Marxism, furthermore, in their ruthlessly organized pursuit of ends—even if desirable ones, even if seemingly inevitable ones—may trample upon or ignore precious individual human resources. To put it within Steinbecks' frame of reference, the Marxists as easily as the banks might be the monsters who send the tractors out. . . .

In light of this interpretation, it is significant that the strike leader in *The Grapes of Wrath*, Jim Casy, is not a Communist. If Casy has a philosophy, it is some version of Emersonian transcendentalism ("Says he foun' he jus' got a little piece of a great big soul," which in turn Tom Joad inherits. And Tom's final vision, it must be repeated, is to have a little piece of land to work for himself. In brief summary, what this means is that in the labor-conflict portions of *The Grapes of Wrath*, Steinbeck uses a Marxian-inspired pattern, but into it he introduces a general, "softer," personally satisfying philosophy, refusing the programmatic one of "hard" Marxism. . . .

Yet Steinbeck could have ended the book there, I repeat, and served his basic theme. To have done so, however, as I have tried to show, would have meant doing violence to many of his deeply felt values. The ending of *The Grapes of Wrath* is, therefore, in some sense an "evasion." Steinbeck's dilemma, however—his ambivalence—was an honest one: the need to protest man's inhumanity to man was strong in him as he wrote *The Grapes of Wrath*, but the two solutions to that oldest of problems which his time presented to him as the most persuasive available, nevertheless implied a direction from which he shrank. Is this dilemma so strange, or his "evasion" so dishonorable? The problem of how to order the public life so as to release the individual into his full dignity and humanity has thus far in the world's history yielded no easy solution. We can scarcely blame Steinbeck for refusing to place all his eggs in the basket of a more and more centralized, highly organized, planned society. However much logic may have directed this step, some deeper, intuitive distrust made him reject it. And who can say that history has not absolved him? Steinbeck ends his book on a quiet note: that life can go on, and that people can and must succour one another. If this is an "evasion" of some of the social, political, and ideological directions in the novel, then I suggest that it is an honest, honorable, and even prophetic one.

CHAPTER 2

Major Themes in *The Grapes of Wrath*

READINGS ON
THE GRAPES OF WRATH

Tom Joad as Epic Hero

Leonard Lutwack

Leonard Lutwack asserts that Tom Joad's heroism takes on mythic proportions after his final meeting with Ma. According to Lutwack, Steinbeck was unable to depict the protagonists of his previous novels as heroic; but given momentum by the powerful twin influences of Ma Joad and Jim Casy, Tom Joad becomes a hero for the twentieth century. Leonard Lutwack has taught at the University of Maryland and is the author of *Birds in Literature* and *The Role of Place in Literature.*

Produced by the influences of a Christ-like companion, Casy, and his mother-goddess, Tom Joad is indeed a hero of divine origin. He is moved to heroic acts by the spirit of anger and revenge which the murder of Casy stirs in him, and on the other hand by the spirit of compassion and love for mankind which his mother so well demonstrates in her selfless devotion to the family. Images of death and rebirth mark Tom's relations with Casy and Ma Joad, as in their different ways they strive to bring him to the role of a hero. There is something terribly grim and sad about the career of Tom. Never allowed a romantic interlude, he is plunged into the troubles of his people upon his return from prison and slowly comes to an awareness of his responsibilities of leadership. Almost glumly, with little expression of personal feeling, he does not only what is expected of him but more besides. A peak in his development occurs when, in the manner of a classic brother-in-arms, Tom at once kills the strikebreaker who has killed Casy; Tom is then himself struck, escapes from his pursuers, and comes to an irrigation ditch, where he bathes his torn cheek and nose. Casy, when he was a preacher, used to baptize people in irrigation ditches; he is killed as he stands beside a stream. Tom's introduction to the bitter struggle of worker against producer

Reprinted from Leonard Lutwack, *Heroic Fiction: The Epic Tradition and American Novels of the Twentieth Century,* by permission of Southern Illinois University Press.
Copyright © 1971 by Southern Illinois University Press.

dates from the violent experience beside the stream. The stinging baptism at the irrigation ditch, after he has fled, does not lead him into his new life at once, however. He must die before he can be wholly reborn, and he must make a retreat to consecrate himself to the cause in his soul as well as in his arm and receive the blessing of his goddess-mother as well as the example of his surrogate father. He re-joins the family, but because he is being sought by the police and can easily be identified by his wounds, he must remain hidden: he is as one who no longer exists in the Joad family. To get past the guards who are looking for him, he lies be-tween two mattresses in the Joad truck, and then he takes refuge in the brush near the boxcar that the family is now inhabiting. After Ruthie has told her playmates about her big brother Tom, Ma decides that she must release Tom from his obligation to the family for his own safety, and she goes to the "cave of vines" he has improvised. Tom, in the mean-time, has come around to a sense of his duty to "fight so hungry people can eat" and is ready to begin a new life away from the family.

MA AND TOM PART: A CLIMACTIC SCENE

The scene in which Ma and Tom part is the climax of Tom's career as a hero and the very heart of Steinbeck's point that class must replace family as the social unit worth fighting for. It is a high point in Steinbeck's writing, and some of its strength comes from the association of rebirth imagery and myths of the mother-goddess and her hero son with the crude story of an organizer of farm labor in twentieth-century America. Carrying a dish of "pork chops and fry potatoes," Ma walks at night "to the end of the line of tents" in the camp of fruit pickers and steps "in among the willows beside the stream" until she reaches "the black round hole of the culvert where she always left Tom's food." She leaves her package at the hole and waits a little distance away, among the willows:

> And then a wind stirred the willows delicately, as though it tested them, and a shower of golden leaves coasted down to the ground. Suddenly a gust boiled in and racked the trees, and a cricking downpour of leaves fell. Ma could feel them on her hair and on her shoulders. Over the sky a plump black cloud moved, erasing the stars. The fat drops of rain scattered down, splashing loudly on the fallen leaves, and the cloud moved on and unveiled the stars again. Ma shivered. The

wind blew past and left the thicket quiet, but the rushing of the trees went on down the stream.

A "dark figure" finally appears at the culvert; it is Tom and after her plea to talk with him he leads Ma to his hideout, across a stream and a field filled with "the blackening stems" of cotton plants. Ma crawls into the "cave of vines" and there in the dark they talk. She explains that she did not let him go earlier because she was afraid for him; with the touch of her hand she discovers that he has a bad scar on his face and his nose is crooked. Again, as in the first scene of recognition between mother and son, the hand of the mother lingers lovingly on the face of the son, just as Thetis [mother of Achilles, hero of the *Iliad*] "took her son's head in her arms" before she releases him for battle in book 18 of the *Iliad*. Ma Joad forces her gift of seven dollars on Tom to help him on his perilous way. Full of his new mission in life, he does not respond to the love his mother expresses for him, but simply says, "Good-by." Ma returns to the camp, and Tom presumably will go on to his doom as Casy did before him but also to a sort of immortality for men who have fought for social justice:

> Then I'll be all aroun' in the dark. I'll be ever'where— wherever you look. Wherever they's a fight so hungry people can eat, I'll be there. Wherever they's a cop beatin' up a guy, I'll be there. If Casy knowed, why, I'll be in the way guys yell when they're mad an'—I'll be in the way kids laugh when they're hungry an' they know supper's ready. An' when our folks eat the stuff they raise an' live in the houses they build— why, I'll be there.

This is a kind of immortality that Ma "don' un'erstan'," although it is she who confers it on him by making his heroism possible.

TOM REBORN AS EPIC HERO

It is not enough to say that this wonderful scene is inspired by the New Testament story of Christ's resurrection from the tomb. The "cave of vines" and the tomb are the womb from which the hero is delivered to a new life, but the landscape in Steinbeck's scene is more nearly that of the classical underworld. The nourishing of the hero-son by the earth-goddess mother until he is strong enough to leave her suggests the myth of Ishtar and Tammuz, and the commitment of the son to war and eventual death recalls the sad exchange between Thetis and Achilles. Tom Joad's "death" brings an end to his ordinary existence as one of thousands of Okies; he is reborn into the life of the epic hero, who dooms himself to an early death as soon as he elects a heroic course of action. His consecration is affirmed by his discipleship to Casy and the ritual release performed by his mother. If there is a resurrection, it is the resurrection of Casy in Tom. Tom's rebirth through the agency of Casy and Ma Joad has a striking antecedent in the experience of Henry Fleming in [American writer Stephen] Crane's *Red Badge of Courage.* The change in Henry's attitude toward heroism—from callow sentimentality to a mature sense of its real consequences—is in part wrought by the example of Jim Conklin, another Christ-like figure, and Henry's encounter with death in the forest, alone, and rebirth among his comrades.

The rebirth of Tom as hero is emphasized by the ironical implication of another incident. Shortly after Ma Joad has returned from the stream and the willows, the pregnant Rosasharn distractedly seeks refuge in the very same place, along "the stream and the trail that went beside it." She lies down among the berry vines and feels "the weight of the baby inside her." Not long after this the rains come. Pa Joad and other men in the camp work feverishly to hold back the swollen stream from flooding their miserable living quarters; they build an earth embankment, but it is swept away and the water washes into the camp. At the same time Ma Joad and some neighboring women are helping Rosasharn deliver her baby, but they meet with no greater success—the baby is stillborn. Uncle John is delegated to bury the "blue shriveled little mummy"; instead, he takes the apple box it is in and floats it down the river, hoping that it will be a sign to the California landowners of the Okies' sore affliction. "Go down an' tell 'em," he says, in words echoing the Negro spiritual "Go Down, Moses" and thus linking three oppressed peoples—Israelites, American Negro slaves, and the Okies. The river is the same that saw the rebirth of Tom, who is a kind of Moses to his people, and now it receives the dead infant.

A TWENTIETH-CENTURY HERO

In Tom the biblical and epic traditions of the hero came together to make a proletarian leader of the twentieth century. The man of anger and the quick blow of revenge is also the disciple devoted to self-sacrifice in the cause of the downtrodden and deprived. The son of the spouse-goddess is released from the death that is the family in order to do battle for the class that will possess the future. The man of violence bred from personal pride—Tom killed his first man in a tavern brawl—is baptized in the violence of class struggle, and he turns, like the classical hero, from the defense of his own rights to the defense of all men's rights. . . .

A NEW COMMUNITY

The Grapes of Wrath begins with a drought bringing death to the land and dispossession to its inhabitants and ends ironically with a flood that again destroys the land and disperses the people. Nature as well as society dooms the Okies, who fall from one catastrophe into another, losing their land, their belongings, their livelihood, and finally even their miserable shelters. But in spite of homelessness and despair, the Joads have succeeded in making an important journey, passing from one bond, the family, to another, mankind. "They's changes—all over," it is said. "Use' ta be the fambly was fust. It ain't so now. It's anybody." In place of the family a new form of social organization is tentatively envisioned on the model of a small socialist community. Not all can see the promised land—only Casy, who does not live to enter it, and Tom, who is on the verge of entering it at the close of the book. Pa Joad's symbolical attempt, in fighting the river, to unite the community after the old style of neighborly cooperation comes too late and fails. Having long since relinquished control of the family to Ma, Pa Joad is a man without a role to play in the world. He joins Magnus Derrick [a character in American novelist Frank Norris's *The Octopus*] in the company of those in the older generation who, unable to accommodate themselves to a new situation, are only pitifully heroic. Others, those who seek individual solutions, are shown to be equally futile. Muley Graves stays on the abandoned farmlands in Oklahoma and must live "like a coyote" on the trash left behind and the wild animals still surviving on the plains. Uncle Noah wanders away down a river he half-wittedly fancies, and Uncle John gets drunk when he can sneak the money. Al, Tom's younger brother, strikes out for himself, ironically to start another hapless family. While Ma cannot understand Tom's social idealism, she and Rosasharn do come around to the side of humanity in the closing scene of the book when Rosasharn, with her mother's prompting, feeds to a dying old man, a stranger, the milk her body had stored for her child. With neither child nor husband Rosasharn must abandon the idea of family. Ma's family has disintegrated, Rosasharn's has not even had a chance to begin.

The images of the community and the hero that dominate the ending of *The Grapes of Wrath* are pitiful enough: a fugitive coming out of hiding to do unequal battle with an infinitely superior enemy and two frightened women trying desperately to save a dying old man in an empty barn. It seems to be an image of miserable survival in the face of awesome odds. Still, out of the sordid circumstances of a purely naturalistic life a hero is born in a manner reminiscent of great heroes of the past. The affirmation of a better future seems groundless, but there is affirmation nonetheless, and a hero is ready to attempt its achievement by leading people who have prepared themselves for a new kind of society. "The book is neither riddle nor tragedy," insists Warren French, "it is an epic comedy of the triumph of the 'holy spirit.'"

STEINBECK'S PREVIOUS FAILED HEROES

Steinbeck seems to want to believe in heroic behavior and the ideal community, yet in one novel after another he submits a negative report as to the chances of either in our time. His first novel, *Cup of Gold* (1929), in Warren French's summary, "asserts that there is no place for the swashbuckling hero in the modern world." In *Tortilla Flat* (1935) Steinbeck lovingly presents the irregular habits and amusing antics of a number of paisanos, but at the same time, by stressing a mock-heroic parallel with [British writer Thomas] Malory's *Morte d'Arthur*, he insists upon our viewing their attempts to be heroic as ridiculous. In the end, Danny, the Arthur of a paisano Round Table, armed with a broken table leg, goes out to do battle and dies in a duel with "The Enemy" in the "gulch," a place which he and his companions used for want of an outhouse. Although the hero in the next novel, *In Dubious Battle* (1936), bears a slight resemblance to another figure from the Arthurian legend, Percival, the mood of this work is starkly naturalistic. Jim Nolan's attempt to become the leader of embattled laborers is soon ended by the blast of a shotgun that renders him, horribly and quite literally, a hero without a face. His epitaph is spoken by his mentor,

Mac, and is necessarily brief: "Comrades! He didn't want nothing for himself—." Lennie, the hero in *Of Mice and Men* (1937), is a feebleminded giant, "shapeless of face," and obviously incapable of responsible behavior. In his time of trouble he takes refuge in a place near a river where a path winds "through the willows and among the sycamores." But Lennie is not reborn there; his best friend must become his executioner there because Lennie cannot control the great strength he has and is consequently a menace to the community.

TOM AS A TRUE HERO

In *The Grapes of Wrath,* for the first time, Steinbeck offers a not altogether forlorn image of the epic hero. Tom Joad is a hero with a face, badly battered though it is; he survives the assault upon him, his spirit is revived at a place where willows grow by a stream and, presumably, he is embarked upon a heroic career. . . .

Tom returns from the cave and the willows, the place of death, to present the face of a hero to the world, a face so badly scarred that he can no longer be recognized as Tom Joad. Of all Steinbeck's heroes, he is the only one who affirms the possibility of a hero arising out of the anonymity of twentieth-century economic strife and still bearing the signs of an ancient dedication.

California as a False Eden

Louis Owens

Louis Owens examines the way Steinbeck employs the myth of the Garden of Eden in *The Grapes of Wrath*. California seems perfect from afar, but when the Joads arrive, it proves to be a false Eden, and the family must adapt to survive. While some have seen the Joads as purely innocent societal victims, Owens suggest that the Joads and all "Okies" have caused many of their own problems through selfishness. The Joads must trade their self-interest and reliance on old myths for a new form of caring and commitment. Louis Owens has taught at the University of New Mexico. In addition to his numerous writings on Steinbeck, he is a critic of Native American literature and the author of the novels *Nightland* and *The Sharpest Sight*.

Central to *The Grapes of Wrath* is Steinbeck's continued preoccupation with California as the ultimate symbol of the American Eden, and in this novel the Great Central Valley of California becomes the microcosm of the new Garden. Once again, a California valley is an ironic, fallen Eden, and the old dream of Eden is rejected in favor of a new dream of commitment. A dazzling cornucopia, the Central Valley lures the migrants westward from Oklahoma and the entire Dust Bowl region with the dream of the Promised Land, the same dream that drove their forebears across the Atlantic and across the continent. The journey of the Joads and the other migrants represents both a social phenomenon of the thirties and a recapitulation of the American westering movement with its echoes of the biblical journey toward Canaan—what Lester Marks has termed the "chosen people" motif of the book. Recognizing this obvious Exodus theme, [critic] Agnes

Reprinted from Louis Owens, *John Steinbeck's Re-Vision of America*, by permission of the University of Georgia Press, © 1985.

McNeill Donohue has equated Steinbeck with [American writer Nathaniel] Hawthorne here, claiming that both "as inheritors of the Puritan tradition use the journey as a complex symbol of fallen man's compulsive but doomed search for Paradise and ritual reenactment of the Fall." While Donohue is correct in placing Steinbeck in the Puritan tradition in his obsession with the quest or journey theme, her interpretation, along with those of most other critics, fails to recognize the fact that for the first time in American literature an author has set out not only to demonstrate the fatal delusion implied in the Eden myth in America, but, more significantly, to replace that myth with a more constructive and attainable dream, the dream of commitment. . . . Whereas many authors—including Hawthorne, [Herman] Melville, [Henry] James, even [F. Scott] Fitzgerald—have offered visions of the danger inherent in the American Dream, only Steinbeck unhesitatingly offers to light the way out of this "doomed Paradise."

Finally, in *The Grapes of Wrath*, the myth that Steinbeck pursued and tested and systematically rejected for nearly a decade comes face to face with a crushing reality: Eden has been reached—one can go no farther westward on the American continent—and Eden has been found corrupt and indisputably fallen, the rotten fruit of the delusive myth upon which the nation was founded. All of Steinbeck's California fiction, all of his fiction to the time of this novel, points toward this final confrontation between myth and reality in the California Eden.

AN AMERICAN WASTELAND

From the first pages of this novel we are faced with another American wasteland, another version of the master symbol given to the twenties by [poet] T.S. Eliot. Critics have generally failed to note, however, the stylistic dexterity with which Steinbeck simultaneously introduces this dustbowl wasteland and subtly foreshadows the structure of the entire novel in the opening paragraphs and first chapter of *The Grapes of Wrath*.

Paragraph one of the novel opens with an impressionistic swath of color reminiscent of [American author] Stephen Crane as Steinbeck intones, "To the red country and part of the gray country of Oklahoma, the last rains came gently, and they did not cut the scarred earth." He continues:

> The plows crossed and recrossed the rivulet marks. The last rains lifted the corn quickly and scattered weed colonies and grass along the sides of the roads so that the gray country and

the dark red country began to disappear under a green cover. In the last part of May the sky grew pale and the clouds that had hung in high puffs for so long in the spring were dissipated. The sun flared down on the growing corn day after day until a line of brown spread along the edge of each green bayonet. The clouds appeared, and went away, and in a while they did not try any more. The weeds grew darker green to protect themselves, and they did not spread any more. The surface of the earth crusted, a thin hard crust, and as the sky became pale, so the earth became pale, pink in the red country and white in the gray country.

A close look at this paragraph shows that following the panoramic, generalized opening, the paragraph begins to focus, to zoom in: "The plows crossed and recrossed the rivulet marks." And finally, from the impressionistic opening image our vision has closed the distance to focus very closely on not just "the growing corn" but the "line of brown" that spreads "along the edge of each green bayonet." At once the camera's eye begins to move back to register broader detail of clouds and generalized "weeds" until the paragraph ends where it began, with a panoramic image of the earth, which "became pale, pink in the red country and white in the gray country." In the second paragraph, the narrative eye again zooms in for a closeup: "In the water-cut gullies the earth dusted down in dry little streams. Gophers and ant lions started small avalanches." And again this paragraph expands to end with panorama: "The air was thin and the sky more pale; and every day the earth paled."

A PATTERN OF EXPANSION AND CONTRACTION

In these first paragraphs Steinbeck introduces the pattern upon which *The Grapes of Wrath* will be structured: a pattern of expansion and contraction—of a generalized, panoramic view of the plight of the migrants followed by a closeup of the plight of representative individuals, the Joads. Furthermore, here Steinbeck brings into the novel a naturalistic image central to the opening chapters, the ant lion. The minuscule trap of an ant lion is a funnel of finely blown dust or sand, a fact of nature from which the ant—struggle as he will—cannot escape. Similarly, the migrants cannot overcome the dust trap of the drought; the fact that they are dusted out is something they are powerless to alter and must simply accept. They must go on the road; there is no choice.

SHARECROPPERS MUST SHARE THE BLAME

The influence of T.S. Eliot and the wasteland theme is first markedly apparent in Steinbeck's writing in the wasted land of *To a God Unknown,* and here, in the blowing, cropped-out earth and shriveled vegetation of the Dust Bowl, Steinbeck presents us with an even more powerful symbol of failed responsibility. Regardless of his professed admiration for the "Okies," not for a moment does Steinbeck exempt the sharecroppers from their portion of blame for the ruined and impotent earth. Like Americans for centuries before them, they have used up the land and now must move west following the archetypal American path. They have "cottoned out" [destroyed the vitality of] the earth from which they derive their physical and psychological sustenance. Here, in what one critic has mistakenly termed "the land of innocence," the sharecroppers plead with the owners of the land for the chance to hang on—maybe there will be a war: "Get enough wars and cotton'll hit the ceiling." They are willing to barter death for a chance to further exploit the land. . . . The farmers have not learned the all-important lesson to be taught in this book: that spiritual and even physical survival depend upon commitment to a larger whole, to "the one inseparable unit man plus his environment." The sharecroppers of the Dust Bowl have failed in their responsibility to the land, and they are sent on the road to learn a new commitment to one another and to the place they will eventually claim in a new land.

A PATTERN OF DESTRUCTION AND ABANDONMENT

Steinbeck aligns the migrants firmly with the mainstream of American history and the American myth when he causes the characters to declare at various times that their fathers had to "kill the Indians and drive them away"; and when the tenants exclaim, "Grampa killed Indians, Pa killed snakes for the land," we should hear a clear echo of the Puritans who wrested the wilderness from the serpent Satan and had to kill many Indians in the process. Though the tenants have tried to persuade the owners to let them hang on, hoping for a war boom in cotton, the tenant-voice also warns the owners: "But you'll kill the land with cotton." And the owners reply, "We know. We've got to take cotton quick before the land dies. Then we'll sell the land. Lots of families in the East would like to own a piece of land." It is the westering pattern of

American history laid bare: drive the Indians and serpent from the Promised Land only to discover that the Garden must lie yet farther to the west. Reject the poor land, use up the good and move on, destroying the Garden in the delusive belief that the Garden has not yet been found. The barren remnants or the unproductive soil are left for those who come behind. The Joads are firmly fixed in this pattern of displacement, and they have no choice but to follow the pattern until, along with the thousands of other migrants, they reach the barrier of the Pacific. It is the pattern which left Old Virginia farmed out by tobacco and which still today lures thousands of Americans westward to the deserts of Arizona, New Mexico, Nevada, and southern California.

EDEN AS FALSE MYTH

The Eden symbolism in *The Grapes of Wrath* is prominent from the novel's first chapter to its last. The owners tell the tenants in Oklahoma, "Why don't you go on west to California? There's work there, and it never gets cold. Why, you can reach out anywhere and pick an orange." And the paean to California sounds again and again until the Joads reach the Golden State. Only Tom is aware from the first that California may not be the Edenic haven they are seeking. Very early, he tells Ma about a Californian who had told him the truth: "He says theys too many folks lookin' for work right there now. An' he says the folks that pick the fruit live in dirty ol' camps an' don't hardly get enough to eat. He says wages is low an' hard to get any." Tom, however, is a pragmatist above all else, a man who says, "I climb fences when I got fences to climb." He realizes that the family has no choice but to move west, that they are trapped in the pattern, so he suppresses his foreknowledge and concentrates on getting the family to California. When they at least reach California, he again establishes a realistic perspective, looking at the mountainous desert waste near Needles and exclaiming, "Never seen such tough mountains. This here's the bones of a country." When Pa protests, "Wait till we get to California. You'll see nice country then," Tom punctures this illusion with "Jesus Christ, Pa! This here *is* California." While not a defeatist, Tom, like Melville's Ishmael, is "quick to perceive a horror." He is the "balanced" man of whom Melville wrote in *Moby-Dick*, the man who will eventually grow to become a leader of the people and who does not succumb to illusion or myth.

What hope and enduring strength is to be found in this novel comes precisely from this ability to pierce the surface and see the ugly reality beneath the façade of the Eden myth and still maintain and nourish a belief in the future.

The male Joads undergo a ritual cleansing in the Colorado River before making the desert crossing into the Garden of the Central Valley, but even during this casual baptism, reality intrudes in the form of a father and son returning from California. While the men are soaking in the river, these defeated Okies tell the Joads, "She's a nice country. But she was stole a long time ago." From the beginning, the reality of the Joads' situation and of the cultural pattern in which they are caught up has undercut any possibility of a new Eden to the west. Others have gone before them; there can be no unspoiled Garden. Only ignorance of the destructive pattern of which they are a part allows the Joads to naïvely expect a Promised Land in the West. . . .

IMAGERY OF THE PROMISED LAND

Nowhere in American literature does California so magnificently fulfill its role of Promised Land as in the scene in which the Joads are introduced to the Central Valley. They stop the old truck atop Tehachapi Pass to look down the valley. It is dawn, the hour of rebirth: "They drove through Tehachapi in the morning glow, and the sun came up behind them, and then—suddenly they saw the great valley below them. Al jammed on the brakes and stopped in the middle of the road, and, 'Jesus Christ! Look!' he said. The vineyards, the orchards, the great flat valley, green and beautiful, the trees set in rows, and the farm houses." Pa's exclamation, "God Almighty!" is followed by a second catalogue: "The distant cities, the little towns in the orchard land, and the morning sun, golden on the valley." And the paean, reminiscent of Whitman, goes on: "The grain fields golden in the morning, and the willow lines, the eucalyptus trees in rows." And, "The peach trees and the walnut groves, and the dark green patches of oranges. And red roofs among the trees, and barns—rich barns." And finally, "The distance was thinned with haze, and the land grew softer and softer in the distance. A windmill flashed in the sun, and its turning blades were like a little heliograph, far away. Ruthie and Winfield looked at it, and Ruthie whispered, 'It's California!'" Winfield brings the Promised Land into focus with the final comment: "There's fruit."

In this heavily stylized hymn to the Promised Land, all of the possibilities inherent in the dream of a new Eden, from the distant vision of Captain John Smith to the Joads' precarious present, rush to fulfillment. We have indeed been allowed our Pisgah view of the New Canaan [Moses' view of the Promised Land], a Garden rediscovered. And, appropriately, once again we encounter a serpent at the edge of Paradise. As the Joads begin to descend toward the valley in the rattletrap truck, "A rattlesnake crawled across the road and Tom hit it and broke it and left it squirming." The path into Paradise has been cleared, and Tom, echoing America's founders and perhaps thinking of the dead grandparents, exclaims, "Jesus, are we gonna start clean! We sure ain't bringin' nothin' with us." It is the archetypal American Dream, and it would appear that the migrants have been reborn in the New Paradise.

A DREAM DESTROYED

It is with this descent into the rich garden of the valley, however, that the fortunes of the Joads, grim thus far, begin their downward flight toward the utter destitution with which the novel ends. Eden proves to be corrupted, its fruit of scientific knowledge rotting in fields and orchards, its lands lying fallow in the ownership of corporations and millionaires, its people divided and frightened and dangerous. And Steinbeck underscores the failure of the American Dream with heavy irony, describing the spring in California in rhapsodic tones recalling the time of "flowering and growth" in [his novel] *The Wayward Bus:*

> The spring is beautiful in California. Valleys in which the fruit blossoms are fragrant pink and white waters in a shallow sea. Then the first tendrils of the grapes swelling from the old gnarled vines, cascade down to cover the trunks. Then the full green hills are round and soft as breasts. . . . All California quickens with produce, and the fruit grows heavy, and the limbs bend gradually under the fruit.

And when the fruit rots in the fields and orchards, Steinbeck takes on the voice of a modern Jeremiah [biblical prophet] to cry, "There is a crime here that goes beyond denunciation. There is a sorrow here that weeping cannot symbolize. There is a failure here that topples all our successes." The jeremiad ends with the warning, "In the souls of the people the grapes of wrath are filling and growing heavy." In the end, when

Rose of Sharon offers her breast to the starving man, she is fulfilling the promise of nature which has been evoked in this description of spring, the season of rebirth. . . .

LESSONS TO BE LEARNED

What the migrants must learn is to rely on the group above and beyond the individual, and to accept responsibility for all men rather than merely for the self or family. As [critic] Warren French has suggested, the migrants must learn to expand their consciousness and sense of responsibility beyond a "reductionist concept of 'family.'" This process of expansion begins when the family takes in Casy, continues with the inclusion of the Wilsons, and culminates in Rose of Sharon's proffered breast. Again, the lesson is that which is central to Steinbeck's fiction: commitment to the whole. . . .

A rebirth of consciousness is taking place throughout this novel as the Joads and other migrants shed their ties to the past and to the cultural pattern that put them on the road to California. The strongest ties to the old land for the Joads are severed when the grandparents die. Connie's desertion cuts away the only believer in the modern version of the American Dream—the illusory futures promised in magazine correspondence courses. The loss of Noah, who walks off down the bank of the Colorado River at the edge of Paradise, symbolizes an even more crucial severance, for Noah's name recalls the Old Testament myth of man's rebirth, or salvation from the doomed, corrupt world. With the disappearance of Noah, a symbolic link to the old mythical structure is cut; now survival for the migrants will depend not on divine intervention to save them from the flood that comes, but on mutual commitment. Emphasis has shifted from the Old Testament, with its Eden myth, to the New Testament and an emphasis upon the commitment symbolized by Christ. Finally, it is Rose of Sharon's stillborn child that symbolizes both the ultimate break with the old myth and the greatest hope for the future of the migrants and, in them, of mankind. Donohue suggests that "the child born to Rose of Sharon is no redeemer, but a stillborn messenger of death. In the fallen Eden of John Steinbeck, no redeemer comes." However, the dead infant does serve as a kind of redeemer in this novel. It is, paradoxically, a symbol of rebirth and hope in the tradition of the vegetation cults that Steinbeck evoked in *To a God Unknown*. Like Adonis and other sacrificial deities, the infant undergoes a kind of "death by water" to prepare for new life. At the same time, in Uncle John's act of sending the dead child downstream in the apple box with the words, "Go down an' tell 'em," we cannot fail to see a stillborn Moses; or, as Donohue says, a "messenger of death." Like the loss of Noah (who, symbolically at least, would have certainly come in handy during the great flood), the dead Moses symbolizes the death of the old myth—there will be no further need for a Moses, for there is nowhere for the migrants to go. They are in the Promised Land already, and they must learn to survive both physically and spiritually in the place where they are. The dead child serves notice that the people will wander no longer.

Tom's Rebirth

Tom is reborn at this point in the novel to replace the rejected Moses as the leader of the people. As John Ditsky has pointed out, Tom is separated completely from his past in the "coal-black cave of vines" where he has hidden. From this womb of nature, Tom is reborn as a new kind of leader who, like Casy, is committed to the people as a whole and to the place these people inhabit now, be it good or bad. Tom will help his people forge a garden from the inhospitable paradise in which they find themselves, but he will not lead them toward an illusory Promised Land that does not exist. In the words of Peter Lisca, Tom has completed the "movement from escape to commitment."

On the literal level, the infant's death prepares for the powerful symbol of commitment—the proffered breast—upon which the novel will end. It prepares for Rose of Sharon's surprisingly sudden conversion from pathetic self-interest to a broadened consciousness and commitment to life as a whole, symbolized by the unknown old man. The archetypal "caritas" [charity] of the final scene symbolizes this commitment. It is important to note here that Rose of Sharon's increasing identification with Ma Joad is designed to prepare her for this new role. When Donohue argues that the Joads' exodus "out of the wilderness to the land of promise is a journey of initiation into dark knowledge, from life to death," she is ignoring an important element of the journey. The Joads' exodus is from the fatal delusion of the American myth, with its inherent denial of commitment, into a knowledge that leads to commitment. It is a journey toward a mystical and non-teleological [the concept that there is no design to the universe] commitment leading to a pragmatic ability to survive in the American Eden that never was.

The novel does not carry the migrants, as another critic suggests, "from the innocence of the Oklahoma chapters, to the experience of the highway and California episodes to the higher innocence of the closing scenes," for while the migrants are for a long time naïve, they are never innocent, especially in the midst of their self-created wasteland. And in the end they are pragmatically committed to the survival of the whole of which they are integral parts. Nor can we say simply that the theme of the final scene and of the novel is that "the prime function of life is to nourish life." For the primary message of the novel is much more complex; it is that the old values and the old myths are dangerously, even fatally, delusive and must be discarded to clear the way for a new commitment to mankind and place, here and now.

Ma Joad as Thematic Center

John H. Timmerman

John H. Timmerman contends that Ma Joad is the central focus of *The Grapes of Wrath.* She holds the family together during the trip west, and, as the males in the novel die, abandon responsibility, or run off, Ma Joad becomes the leader of those who remain. Ma Joad is notable for her generosity and her patience— in the face of mounting troubles, she is still able to nurture and feed others. John H. Timmerman has taught at Calvin College in Grand Rapids, Michigan. He has written book-length studies of Steinbeck and T.S. Eliot, and his works of fiction include *The Forgotten Wise Man* and *Valley of the Shadow.*

Between the poles of Tom Joad and Jim Casy, Ma Joad is the lodestar that evinces calm and grants direction. Her concept of the family of man, which she holds intuitively from the start, is the final point at which the others arrive like grim pilgrims, knowing the place for the first time. The enigmatic ending of the novel in this instance is indeed a thematic fulfillment, and it is no wonder that Steinbeck fought his editors to retain it. Strip away that ending and one destroys the thematic structure of the novel. The ending represents the direction Ma Joad has been traveling since the start of the novel, and it is no accident that Rose of Sharon's action occurs at Ma Joad's behest. But to arrive properly at that ending, we consider first the character development of Ma Joad in relation to the thematic development—this woman who says, "'I ain't got faith,'" but whose faith finally proves sufficient to undergird the whole family.

Ma Joad as a Feeder

Ma Joad is typified from the outset by a generosity that, along with patient loving-kindness, will guide her actions in

Excerpted from *John Steinbeck's Fiction: The Aesthetics of the Road Taken*, by John H. Timmerman, by permission of the publisher, the University of Oklahoma Press, © 1986.

relation to the family of man throughout. She is, in a sense, the female counterpart to Doc Burton [a character in Steinbeck's *In Dubious Battle*] in her steadfast performance of altruistic deeds. When Pa Joad plays his little trick of introducing Tom and Casy as strangers, "'Ma, there's a couple fellas jus' come along the road, an' they wonder if we could spare a bite,'" Ma's reaction is immediate: "'Let 'em come. . . . We got a'plenty.'" That they do not have a'plenty is undeniable, but not as undeniable as the need of others that Ma will always try to meet. This idea of the woman as matriarchal "Feeder" is important in twentieth-century southern fiction and characteristic of real migrant families on their long pilgrimage to California. The father is the worker-provider, the mother the nourisher-feeder—source of spiritual as well as physical nourishment.

Among the migrants Steinbeck would, no doubt, have witnessed the "feeder" ritual dozens of times. . . .

A FEEDING SCENE

Steinbeck himself records one such scene in *The Grapes of Wrath* at the first California migrant camp. The scene is preceded by intercalary chapter 19, which raises the cry of hunger as a backdrop: "How can you frighten a man whose hunger is not only in his own cramped stomach but in the wretched bellies of his children? You can't scare him—he has known a fear beyond every other." In chapter 20 the Joads find the reality of the intercalary chapter at the Hooverville camp. Over and over the refrain rises: "'S'pose they's a hundred men wants that job. S'pose them men got kids, an' them kids is hungry. S'pose a lousy dime'll buy a box a mush for them kids. S'pose a nickel'll buy at leas' somepin for them kids.'" And in the center of that raging hunger Ma Joad fixes the family meal, while the camp children watch with wolfish eyes: "The children, fifteen of them, stood silently and watched. And when the smell of the cooking stew came to their noses, their noses crinkled slightly." Finally Ma, the Feeder and Nourisher, ladles out her stew for the others, saying as she does so, "'I can't send 'em away . . . I don't know what to do.'" This same Feeder motif operates at the end of the novel, where Ma asks Rose of Sharon to give her breast to the starved man, an ending structurally and thematically anticipated from the first meeting with Ma Joad.

MA JOAD'S STRENGTH

Gradually, in the development of the novel, as the men are torn between the "I" and the "we", Ma Joad also takes over the dominant male role of the family so that her generosity and loving-kindness will prevail. She is no one's apathetic servant. As Feeder, she must be indomitably strong, for if the Feeder weakens, the family falls apart. Her fight is for the family—and indeed for the family of man—rather than for herself.

Ma Joad is not immune to the sense of catastrophe and of hope mixed with fear, that accompanies the migrant exodus. In fact, she finds some solace in the sheer numbers of people leaving, and at one point she anticipates the war cry of the California migrant camps:

> She came near to him then, and stood close; and she said passionately, "Tommy, don't you go fightin' 'em alone. They'll hunt you down like a coyote. Tommy, I got to thinkin' an' dreamin' an' wonderin'. They say there's a hundred thousand of us shoved out. If we was all made the same way, Tommy—they wouldn't hunt nobody down—."

There is steel in this woman's hope. And when hopelessness first begins to descend upon the others, in chapter 16, Ma Joad begins to exert control, threatening Pa with a jack-handle until she gets her way. While Pa gives in with some obligatory curses, Tom questions her: "'What's the matter'th you anyways? You gone johnrabbit on us?'" To which Ma responds: "'You done this 'thout thinkin' much. . . . What we got lef' in the worl'? Nothin' but us. Nothin' but the folks.'" To protect the family she will stand up to anyone, even her own.

Ma's steel-like courage and control are strengthened on the desert crossing. While Connie and Rose of Sharon try in their desperate little privacy to make love, Ma Joad cradles the dying Granma's head in her lap, and even after Granma dies, Ma retains the courage to bluff her way past the border inspection. Spiritually and psychologically she assumes control over the family.

MA JOAD AT WEEDPATCH

The Weedpatch camp poses a crisis for both the psychological well-being of the family and the spiritual control of Ma Joad. Having sojourned in tribulation, having been demeaned by the common epithet "Okies" on the lips of calloused and angry men, the family has its dignity reaffirmed at Weedpatch. Ma sighs, "'Why, I feel like people again.'" The camp is marked by small items that seem to validate human worth: from flush toilets to dances to the dignity of labor as a commodity for barter. And while the dubious battle rages outside the walls of Weedpatch, one feels that one could harbor in its port forever. But ironically Weedpatch has its own pyschological nettles. For example, it robs the people of their will. At ease with their heaven-sent manna, the migrants do not want to risk the struggle into Canaan. In the camp the migrants find themselves becoming more and more dependent, depleted in will and direction. The Joad resources prove insufficient to sustain the family. Ma rises to goad them on, and the argument that rises to meet her is precisely the desirability of being at ease. "'This here hot water an' toilets—'" Pa argues, to which Ma responds, "'Well, we can't eat no toilets.'" Again Ma exerts her authority and issues the command:

> Ma plunged the dish into the bucket. "We'll go in the mornin'," she said.
>
> Pa sniffled. "Seems like times is changed," he said sarcastically. "Time was when a man said what we'd do. Seems like women is tellin' now. Seems like it's purty near time to get out a stick."
>
> Ma put the clean dripping tin dish out on a box. She smiled down at her work. "You get your stick, Pa," she said. "Times when they's food an' a place to set, then maybe you can use your stick an' keep your skin whole."

And again, it is Tom who presses her for her reasons, to which Ma responds:

> Take a man, he can get worried an' worried, an' it eats out his liver an' purty soon he'll jus' lay down and die with his heart et out. But if you can take an' make 'im mad, why, he'll be awright. Pa, he didn't say nothin', but he's mad now. He'll show me now. He's awright.

MA JOAD AS FAMILY HEAD

Yet a third time the issue of control rises, notable here because Ma uses the occasion to reflect on the nature of women. Suffused with a vast loneliness for his old homestead and feeling lost in the new land, Pa Joad exclaims: "'Funny! Woman takin' over the fambly. Woman sayin' we'll do this here, an' we'll go there. An' I don' even care.'" Ma soothes him by responding: "'Woman can change better'n a man. . . . Woman got all her life in her arms. Man got it all in his head. Don' you mind.'" After a short pause Ma adds: "'Man, he lives in jerks—baby born an' a man dies, an' that's a jerk—gets a farm, an' loses his farm, an' that's a jerk. Women, it's all one flow, like a stream, little eddies, little waterfalls, but the river, it goes right on. Woman looks at it like that. We ain't gonna die out. People is goin' on—changin' a little, maybe, but goin' right on.'"

Like [American novelist William] Faulkner's Dilsey in *The Sound and the Fury*, Ma Joad endures; somehow she sees past the fiery emotions of the moment to one sure light that guides her path. In so doing she keeps the dream alive, nurtures and feeds it, of a "fambly" of man united in the same love and generosity she exhibits. The spirit is infectious, in a sense replacing—or perhaps the alternative to—the Group Man infection of the Mob that Doc Burton analyzes in *In Dubious Battle*. In Ma's hour of need, Mrs. Wainwright reciprocates:

> Ma fanned the air slowly with her cardboard. "You been frien'ly," she said. "We thank you."
>
> The stout woman smiled. "No need to thank. Ever'body's in the same wagon. S'pose we was down. You'd give us a han'."
>
> "Yes," Ma said, "we would."
>
> "Or anybody."
>
> "Or anybody. Use' to be the fambly was fust. It ain't so now. It's anybody. Worse off we get, the more we got to do."

A new movement has started, and its beginning—not its ending—is exemplified at the close of the novel as Ma's eyes and Rose of Sharon's meet in acknowledgment:

> "Hush," said Ma. She looked at Pa and Uncle John standing helplessly gazing at the sick man. She looked at Rose of Sharon huddled in the comfort. Ma's eyes passed Rose of Sharon's eyes, and then came back to them. And the two women looked deep into each other. The girl's breath came short and gasping.
>
> She said "Yes."
>
> Ma smiled. "I knowed you would. I knowed!"

From the dust-filled skies of Oklahoma to the rain-laden skies and scudding clouds of California, Ma Joad points a straight path for her family. Similarly she is the thematic center of the novel.

CHAPTER 3

Techniques

READINGS ON
THE GRAPES OF WRATH

Steinbeck's Use of Interchapters

Peter Lisca

One of Steinbeck's more daring strategies in *The Grapes of Wrath* was to insert what he called "interchapters" between episodes in the Joad narrative. These sections interrupt the flow of the novel to make observations—often highly critical—concerning American society during the Great Depression. Some critics, such as Frederick Hoffman, have argued that Steinbeck's interchapters are the weakest part of *The Grapes of Wrath*. Peter Lisca, author of *John Steinbeck: Nature & Myth*, from which this selection is excerpted, defends Steinbeck's strategy. Lisca says that the interchapters broaden the range of the novel and vividly dramatize a social problem of national scope so as to transcend propaganda and give it true artistic merit. The result, Lisca maintains, is a novel of "literary genius" that deserves to be ranked with the great American novels.

Steinbeck is frequently identified as a proletarian writer of the nineteen thirties, one whose dominant interest lay in the social and political problems of the Great Depression. But although *In Dubious Battle* and *Of Mice and Men* might generally seem to justify this reputation, neither work is specifically dated either by its materials or by Steinbeck's treatment. Migrant workers and union organizers had long been part of the California scene—and continued so to be. Steinbeck's early short story, "The Raid" (1934), dealing with two labor organizers, similarly avoids identification with its decade. It was not until 1939, at the very end of the period, that he published *The Grapes of Wrath*, a work clearly and specifically grounded in conditions and events that were then making news. In fact, so directly and powerfully did this novel deal with contemporary events that it itself became an important part of those events—debated in public forums, banned, burned, denounced from pulpits, attacked in pamphlets, and even debated on the floor of Congress. Along with such works as Upton Sinclair's *The Jungle* and Harriet Beecher Stowe's *Uncle Tom's Cabin, The Grapes of Wrath* has achieved a place among those novels that so stirred the American public for a social cause as to have had measurable political impact. Although thus associated with this class of social-protest fiction, *The Grapes of Wrath* continues to be read, not as a piece of literary or social history, but with a sense of emotional involvement and aesthetic discovery. More than any other American novel, it successfully embodies a contemporary social problem of national scope in an artistically viable expression. It is unquestionably John Steinbeck's finest achievement, a work of literary genius. . . .

REALISTIC CHARACTERS

The novel's main characters are the twelve members of the Joad family: Grampa, Granma, Pa, Ma, their children Winfield, Ruthie, Noah, Al, Tom (just returned from prison), Rosasharn and her husband Connie, and Uncle John, joined by the ex-preacher Jim Casy. . . .

All the characters are drawn as fully credible human beings, individual yet also representative of their social class and circumstances. This is true even of such clearly unusual and strong personalities as Tom Joad, Jim Casy, Ma Joad, and her daughter Rosasharn. Casy, although a vision-pierced prophet, retains enough elements of his revival-meeting, "Jesus-jumping" sect and cultural folkways to remain specifically human. Ma Joad's heroic maternal qualities reflect the strength and character of those migrant wives who not only survived but nourished as well their children and husbands. . . . Such details as Grampa's senility, Al's abilities as an automobile mechanic, Connie's faith in cheap, correspondence trade schools, Uncle John's guilt complex, and Rosasharn's pregnancy personalize each character in turn and contribute to the reader's involvement. But Steinbeck was not writing a novel of personal adventure and misfortune. His theme is the entire social condition of which his characters are a part, and it is primarily in terms of the total situation that they have existence. Thus their role is collective, representational of the Okies and migrant workers, just as in the novel the Shawnee Land and Cattle Company represents the evicting landlords, and the California Farmers' Association represents the growers.

THE USE OF INTERCHAPTERS

That Steinbeck succeeds in creating characters capable of bearing such wide responsibility is a brilliant achievement, but the novel's vast subject requires even more. To have put the Joads into the large variety of situations needed to add up to a total picture would have destroyed their necessary credibility as particular and real people. Rather than vastly increasing the number of characters and thus weakening the reader's empathetic response and the novel's narrative line, or digressing from the action with authorial comment, Steinbeck conceived the idea of using alternating chapters as a way of filling in the larger picture. About one hundred pages, or one sixth of the book, is devoted to this purpose. At first glance it might seem that putting these digressions from the Joad family into separate chapters interrupts the narrative line even more, and that such a device breaks the book into two distinct parts, or kinds of chapters, resulting in a monotonous tick tock effect. Of this danger the author was well aware, and he avoided it by using in the interchapters a variety of devices to minimize their interruption of the narrative action, temper their expository nature, and otherwise blend the two kinds of chapters in the reader's mind.

Perhaps the most important of the devices Steinbeck uses is dramatization. Chapter five, for example, deals with the process by which mortgaged lands are taken over by the banks, the small farmers evicted, and these lands combined into vast holdings cultivated with efficient modern machinery by absentee landlords. . . . Steinbeck presents a series of vignettes in which, through generalized characters, situations, and dialogue, we see these things happening. The device is reminiscent of the medieval mystery plays which dramatized Bible stories and made them real to the common people; or of Greek drama which through familiar figures and a chorus of elders or women gave voice to the people's ethical and religious beliefs. Even the introduction and the transitions between these vignettes share this dramatized quality, as in the opening paragraph of chapter five, in which "owners" are presented walking, talking, touching things, and "tenants" are listening, watching, squatting in the dust which they mark with their little sticks, their wives standing in the doorways, the children wriggling their toes. In similar fashion other chapters present further aspects of the total situation: chapter seven, the buying of used cars for the trip; chapter nine, the selling of household goods; chapters seventeen and twenty-three, the nature of migrant life along the road.

JUXTAPOSITION OF CHAPTER AND INTERCHAPTER

Another device that Steinbeck uses to integrate the two kinds of material is juxtaposition. Of course, everything included in the interchapters is related to the events of the narrative. And each interchapter is so placed that its content is most pertinent to the action in the chapter that precedes or follows it. Highway 66 is the subject of the interchapter that follows the Joads' turning onto that highway; the rain and flood of chapter twenty-nine set the stage for the novel's conclusion. But furthermore, and most effectively, the interchapters are frequently used to develop or complete some specific action initiated in the preceding narrative, or vice versa. Chapter eight ends with the Joads driving off to sell their household goods; the interchapter that follows presents us with generalized characters selling just such goods; in chapter ten the Joads return with the empty truck, having sold their goods, pack the truck, and leave home; chapter eleven describes the gradual deterioration of an abandoned house. A variation of this device is achieved by repetition, in which some specific detail in one kind of chapter reappears in the other, thus further knitting the two together. The anonymous house in an interchapter becomes the Joad house when, in the following chapter, the latter also is seen with one of its corners knocked off the foundation; the anonymous man with a rifle who in the same interchapter threatens the tractor driver becomes Grampa Joad, who in the next chapter is reported to have shot out the headlight of a tractor. . . .

A PROBLEM OF NATIONAL DIMENSIONS

All this is not to say that the sixteen interchapters are equally brilliant or successful. Perhaps three of them (nineteen, twenty-one, twenty-five), concerned with historical information, and a few paragraphs in two or three others, are too direct. But these are exceptions. For the most part, the problem raised by the use of interchapters is fully met by the brilliance of Steinbeck's literary technique.

In themselves, then, the interchapters accomplish several things for the novel. As has been mentioned, they provide an artistically acceptable place for the author's own statements, and they make possible the inclusion of additional materials without overusing the Joads or introducing many other specific characters. Closely related to this latter function is these chapters' capacity for amplification. They present dramatically with a sense of real experience what would otherwise be left to inference—that the situations and actions of the Joad family are typical of a large group of people, that the Joads are caught up in a problem of national dimensions. These are perhaps the chapters' most important uses. In addition, they provide information—the history of land ownership and migrant labor in California, for example. Also, through their depiction of American people, scenes, and folkways, there emerges the portrait of a substantial portion of a people—their political and religious beliefs, their music, manners, stories, jokes; their essentially pioneer character, with its virtues and its limitations. *The Grapes of Wrath* is a "great American novel" in every sense of that phrase.

The Forms of *The Grapes of Wrath*

W.M. Frohock

According to W.M. Frohock, two basic, conflicting structures in *The Grapes of Wrath* pull it in opposite directions. The book has the form of a road novel; such novels tend to be disjointed because they are made up of a number of separate episodes occurring in various locations. But the second structure, that of tragedy, holds *The Grapes of Wrath* together and keeps it moving toward the inevitable climactic scenes. Steinbeck's limitation in constructing this tragedy, Frohock concludes, is that he oversimplifies the situation in California by making all of the Okies heroic while all of the Californians are villainous. This flaw mars but does not ruin the novel as a work of art. At his death in 1984, W.M. Frohock was Professor Emeritus of Romance Languages and Literature at Harvard University.

In *The Grapes of Wrath* [the] good, kindhearted, ignorantly immoral irresponsibles become the figures of a tragedy. When they pull up stakes for the long drag from Oklahoma to California, they are pushed on by a force which they understand no better than the Greeks understood fate. We speak of Economic Drives as the Greeks spoke of Gods, but we know only vaguely what urges them along, and the Joads know less than we. We know further that whatever the Joads do they will never be able to escape, and that the little wisps of hope they carry with them, feeble as they are, are unjustified: disaster lies ahead; they hasten to it; they could not turn back if they would.

Their progress hardly stops for the basic processes of life and death. When the old grandfather dies they hurry his body into the ground so that they can be on the way in the

Reprinted from W.M. Frohock, *The Novel of Violence in America* (Dallas: Southern Methodist University Press, 1950), by permission of the Estate of W.M. Frohock.

morning. The grandmother dies on the truck itself while, during her agony, Rose of Sharon and her husband have their way with each other, sprawled on top of the load; the beginning and the end of life alike are unable to delay the course of the tragedy. And meanwhile at the other end of the journey the antagonist is ready. He is animated by the same forces that are driving the Joads, and is no more able to let go what he has than they are to refrain from trying to take it away from him. He is as ignorant as they of what makes them all behave as they do. Finally in the fields and groves of California they come to grips and both sides are defeated, the men of Oklahoma first and within the scope of the book; the people of California later but just as inevitably, as we who are reading realize.

We are left with no feeling that the violence of the novel is an arbitrary thing, put there because to the author violence is beautiful or fascinatingly ugly. Because of the inevitability of the clash, the book has the form of tragedy: like tragedy it points all in one direction; the force is so strong, the flow and sweep of the thing so inescapable, that whatever digression is in it appears as no more than a minor fault and does not obscure the novelist's purpose.

A ROAD-NOVEL

The word "form" as applied to novels is a metaphor, and a different metaphor may make this point clearer: let us say "progression." *The Grapes of Wrath* has the progression of tragedy so completely that the interpolated chapters, which explain events to the reader and which we may think of as choruses, are swept along without deflecting the tragic impetus. This is fortunate, because the book is also a road-novel. The road-novel is a favorite storytelling device to get unity running through a set of adventures which would otherwise bear small relation to one another. Conversely, the frame of the road-novel is an open invitation to episodic writing—the characters are here and something happens, they move to another place and something else happens, etc. When you can remember individual episodes in a novel better than you remember the total effect of the book, the chances are that you have been reading a road-novel, something like [Miguel de Cervantes's] *Don Quixote* or [Henry Fielding's] *Tom Jones* or [Ernest Hemingway's] *The Sun Also Rises,* to name only great ones.

> ### STEINBECK'S FAILED NOVEL
> *In* The Art of Fiction, *well-known novelist John Gardner argues that Steinbeck's simplification of the Californians ruins* The Grapes of Wrath.
>
> No ignoramus—no writer who has kept himself innocent of education—has ever produced great art. One trouble with having read nothing worth reading is that one never fully understands the other side of one's argument, never understands that the argument is an old one (all great arguments are), never understands the dignity and worth of the people one has cast as enemies. Witness John Steinbeck's failure in *The Grapes of Wrath*. It should have been one of America's great books. But while Steinbeck knew all there was to know about Okies and the countless sorrows of their move to California to find work, he knew nothing about the California ranchers who employed and exploited them; he had no clue to, or interest in, their reasons for behaving as they did; and the result is that Steinbeck wrote not a great and firm novel but a disappointing melodrama in which complex good is pitted against unmitigated, unbelievable evil.
>
> John Gardner, *The Art of Fiction.* New York: Vintage Books, 1991.

The tendency of the road-novel to break up into episodes is all the more dangerous to a novelist who tends by nature to write episodically, as does Steinbeck. He can persuade himself that he has put unity into his work where no one else sees it. . . .

THE GRAPES OF WRATH AS TRAGEDY

That the . . . problem of unity did not trap Steinbeck testifies to the inner strength of the tragedy he conceived. I have no desire to make Steinbeck into a rather strained-looking Greek, but it seems to me that he has put into *The Grapes of Wrath* most of the elements of tragedy: the driving forces, the swift rush of events, inevitability, mounting pity and terror, clash, violence. His characters react properly in the face of evil, and the foolish things they do are pieces of eternally human foolishness.

There is a price to pay, however, for the tragedy we get. Steinbeck's compassion leads to oversimplification, a distaste for complication which extends beyond a mere dislike of complicating personalities. For our purposes it is unimportant that the original popularity of *The Grapes of Wrath* was a product of its timeliness and topical interest, that it appeared at a moment when interest in alleviating the lot of the migrants was widespread; the book is no whit greater because, as a reform tract, it did have a practical and beneficial effect on the condition of the Okies and Arkies in California. We do not now read *The Grapes of Wrath* for these reasons. The important thing for us here and now is that the plight of these people raised in Steinbeck the passion and anger which caused him to write the book. In his wrath he goes too far. He can see only two kinds of people, those like the Joads and those who whirl past the migrants on Highway 66 in expensive cars. One page of *The Grapes of Wrath* reveals the violence of the antithesis:

> Languid, heat-raddled ladies, small nucleuses about whom revolve a thousand accouterments: creams, ointments to grease themselves, coloring matter in phials—black, pink, red, white, green, silver—to change the color of hair, eyes, lips, nails, brows, lashes, lids. Oils, seeds, and pills to make the bowels move. A bag of bottles, syringes, pills, powders, fluids, jellies to make their sexual intercourse safe, odorless and unproductive. And this apart from clothes. What a hell of a nuisance! . . . Beside them, little pot-bellied men in light suits and Panama hats; clean, pink men with puzzled, worried eyes, with restless eyes. Worried because formulas do not work out; hungry for security and yet sensing its disappearance from the earth. In their lapels the insignia of lodges and service clubs, places where they can go and, by a weight of numbers of little worried men, reassure themselves that business is noble and not the curious ritualized thievery they know it is; that business men are intelligent in spite of the records of their stupidity; that they are kind and charitable in spite of the principles of sound business; that their lives are rich instead of the thin tiresome routines they know; and that a time is coming when they will not be afraid any more.

STEINBECK'S SIMPLIFICATION OF CHARACTERS

Over against such people Steinbeck sets the honest, jovial vulgarity of men like the transport truck drivers. You must, he implies, be one kind or the other. There is an exclusiveness here that suggests a sort of inverted snobbery; it would seem that one can't qualify as a decent individual unless one can simplify his personality to the point of sharing the ideal expressed by George in *Of Mice and Men:* "When the end of the month come I could take my fifty bucks and go into town and get whatever I want. Why, I could stay in a cat house all night. I could eat any place I want, hotel or any place, and order any damn thing I could think of. An' I could do all that every damn month. Get a gallon of whiskey, or set in a pool room and play cards or shoot pool."

This oversimplification is a pity, not because it spoils *The Grapes of Wrath* (it does not), but because it prevented Steinbeck's writing a book which would have been much more universally American. When the Joads arrive in California and the inevitable clash arises, we see its effect only on one party. We do not get the story of the little people on the other side. Yet the men who fought against the Joads were just as terrified and in the long run just as luckless. When circumstances turn them against their own kind, the plight of the have-a-littles is just as pitiable as that of the have-nots. Steinbeck goes to some lengths to establish our faith in the fact that his people are typically American, not only by introducing the classical rural jokes about sex in the barnyard, but by laboring over the native mysticism of Tom and more especially of Casy, the ex-preacher who can't feel religious without wanting a woman, too. (The mysticism is something many of us could get along without, not because we don't like [American poet] Walt Whitman but because when we want him we know where to get him in the original.) *The Grapes of Wrath* would be symbolically American if the reader had to sympathize with both sides at once, a situation familiar to almost every American of Steinbeck's time. Some of Steinbeck's literary tragedy would have been spoiled in the process, but we would have been thrown face to face with the tragic ambivalence of our lives.

The Drinking Metaphor in *The Grapes of Wrath*

A. Carl Bredahl Jr.

A. Carl Bredahl Jr. traces Steinbeck's use of drink as metaphor: The beverages consumed by the characters roughly correspond to their interactions with others, and Steinbeck uses these drinks metaphorically to suggest the novel's thematic movement from isolation to community. Toward the end of the novel, and particularly in the final scene, Bredahl concludes, Steinbeck uses milk as a symbol of the novel's movement from selfishness to selflessness. A. Carl Bredahl has taught at the University of Florida and written books on Ernest Hemingway and Herman Melville.

In John Steinbeck's *The Grapes of Wrath,* several traditional novel techniques are altered so as to develop the theme and direction of the novel from *I* to *we,* from the individual to the group. The interchapters, for example, repeatedly remind us that the Joads are part of a larger story, just as the breakdown of the Joad family unit is paralleled by a joining of members of several families. Even the methods of characterization support this change. In the opening of the book, characters are striking in their realistic detail. Individual gestures and idiosyncrasies are emphasized, and Grandpa's open trousers and "cantankerous, complaining, mischievous" face become superb examples of Steinbeck's art. But as the book develops, the realism is heightened, and the characters become more romantic as the sharpness of detail is supplanted by a generalizing of common characteristics. In Tom, Ma, Rose of Sharon, even Al, we finally are presented with aspects of man rather than distinct individuals. This same movement outwards applies to the imagery of the novel as well as to its complex of themes. What is particularly interesting is not that the imagery echoes the themes—this is to be expected—but that

Reprinted from A. Carl Bredahl Jr., "The Drinking Metaphor in *The Grapes of Wrath,*" *Steinbeck Quarterly,* vol. 6, no. 4, Fall 1973, pp. 95–98, by permission of the *Steinbeck Quarterly.*

Steinbeck's technique is exactly the same in both cases. This point may be demonstrated by a detailed examination of one specific image—drinking. Steinbeck's concern with food has often been noted, and naturally there is a corresponding reference to drink. But the particular liquids consumed change during the course of the novel, a change which illustrates Steinbeck's technique and which demonstrates the appropriateness of the final scene as the culmination of the book.

FOUR SYMBOLIC LIQUIDS

Four liquids are predominant in *The Grapes of Wrath:* liquor, water, milk, and coffee. Liquor is significant only in the first two-thirds of the book; water is only mentioned in the first half, receiving its main attention on the trip from Oklahoma to California; milk is not mentioned until the second half and is emphasized only in the final hundred pages; coffee is used in general throughout. What is most immediately striking about the occurrences of these references is the fact that three of them are restricted in use to particular sections of the novel, coffee being the only exception. There is no established pattern to the use of coffee other than the fact that, as one might expect, it is usually associated with sociability.

Bottled alcohol receives its major attention in the early section of the novel and, unlike coffee, is associated with isolation. Though the consuming of liquor usually connotes good fellowship, in *The Grapes of Wrath* it is always consumed apart from the group. Tom and Jim Casy share a drink in Chapter 4, but at this point neither of them has developed the group consciousness he later will. Each is a man alone, sitting or walking in a deserted, barren world. Tom offers a drink to the truck driver in Chapter 2 but finally drinks alone; having left the family in Chapter 16 in order to look for a con-rod, Al is anxious to get a beer, but Tom is now more concerned about the group than himself and suggests that they save their money. In Chapter 21 when Uncle John decides to get drunk, he goes off alone. Liquor is also the least natural of the four liquids and, correspondingly, the most sanitary. Something artificially produced, bottled, and sealed is clean but in the sense of sterile. When Tom and Casy drink together, therefore, it is fitting that "Joad [takes] the bottle from him, and in politeness [does] not wipe the neck with his sleeve before he [drinks]." The suggestion here is that cleanliness might be sanitary, as it is for the wealthy Easterners in Chapter 15 who stop for bottled soda, but it is not sociable. In addition, liquor inebriates, deadens the senses, makes one less aware of his world. Tom is drunk when he commits his first murder, but very much awake for the second. And the wine produced in the California fields has "not the rich odor of wine, but the smell of decay and chemicals." Its only value is that it has alcohol in it, and a man can get drunk. What happens then is summed up in Chapter 23.

> And always, if he had a little money, a man could get drunk. The hard edges gone, and the warmth. Then there was no loneliness, for a man could people his brain with friends, and he could find his enemies and destroy them. Sitting in a ditch, the earth grew soft under him. Failures dulled and the future was no threat. And hunger did not skulk about, but the world was soft and easy.

For these several reasons then, because it is isolating, sterile, and inebriating, it is appropriate that alcohol should only be associated with the early sections of the novel when the characters themselves are most isolated and life is most sterile. However, when Tom throws away the bottle in Chapter 4, so does Steinbeck.

In Chapter 6 liquor is replaced by water, and for the next 150 pages water is the major beverage consumed. Like alcohol, water too is clean but in no way sterile, for it is water that is needed to make the dust bowl productive. But while water is necessary for plants, it can only *maintain* human life; it does not provide nourishment. Thus in the Joads' trek across the country, the change from alcohol to water does suggest purification, but it also suggests that human life is simply being sustained. Water hoses are stuck indiscriminately into human mouths and automobile radiators. Yet, man is not a machine; he needs something more than water if he is to remain healthy. It is not surprising, therefore that in this section of the novel, in contrast to the lush countryside of California, Steinbeck introduces sickness and death.

MILK OF HUMAN KINDNESS

The final direction of the book, however, is not toward sickness but toward growth; not just grapes but grapes of wrath are to be harvested. The individual may die, but humanity is to flourish; the Joad family may succumb, but the family of man is to grow. Appropriately, then, milk should replace both liquor and water in the final section of the novel. During the last hundred pages of *The Grapes of Wrath* there are almost a dozen references to milk but none to either liquor or drinking water, and, as one would expect, all of the references to milk are to the nourishment it provides—as, for example, when Winfield gets sick. More significantly, however, in contrast to the isolation which earlier characterized the drinking of liquor, Steinbeck also closely associates milk with self-sacrifice, even if at times it is done grudgingly.

> "Now what?" Pa demanded.
> "It's Winfiel'. He needs some milk."
> "Christ Awmighty! We all need stuff!"
> Ma said, "How much'd we make today?"
> "Dollar Forty-two."
> "Well, you go right over'n get a can a milk for Winfiel'."
> "Now why'd he have to get sick?"
> "I don't know why, but he is. Now you git!" Pa went grumbling out the door.

Self-sacrifice in order to provide nourishment also describes Rose of Sharon's actions at the end. Thus the twin concerns which are at the heart of this novel, nourishment and individual involvement, are brought together in Steinbeck's use of milk. This point is further emphasized by the handling of the flood which closes the book. After the opening of *The Grapes of Wrath*, we are certainly aware of the need for water to revitalize the land. However, as I have already suggested, Steinbeck indicates on a symbolic level that water is insufficient for human growth. The flood dramatically demonstrates this insufficiency, thereby placing greater emphasis upon the need for man's personal involvement with other men.

It is inviting to see the rain as bringing nourishment back to the land, just as Rose of Sharon's milk brings life to the old man. But the Joads are no longer in the Oklahoma dust bowl, and the rain is not eagerly anticipated. "'Looks like we might have a little rain,'" says a stranger to Ma. "'I hope not. Stop the picking'. We need the pickin'!'" Since the Joads are no longer dependent on water, for the crops are flourishing, the rain clouds, once eagerly looked for, are now ominous. The danger is lack of work. The pickers race against the oncoming clouds, and when they finally arrive, Steinbeck's description emphasizes only the destructive aspect of the water.

> And the streams and the little rivers edged up to the bank sides and worked at willows and tree roots bent the willows deep in the current, cut out the roots of cottonwoods and

brought down the trees. The muddy water whirled along the bank sides and crept up the banks until at last it spilled over, into the fields, into the orchards, into the cotton patches where the black stems stood. Level fields became lakes, broad and gray, and the rain whipped up the surfaces.

The greatest terror of all is not the lack of water but that "they ain't gonna be no kinda work for three months." Dust bowl or flood, man can only look to other men. Neither economic systems nor natural forces can provide nourishment. Conversely, systems and floods will not destroy man if he surrenders his selfishness for the welfare of others. Thus the image of drinking and the novel's thematic concerns develop together, both emphasizing the need to move from the isolated *I* to the self-supporting *we*. Neither an artificially produced stimulant nor water is sufficient for man's nourishment. Milk is produced within a living body and given to another living body in a giving of self. Only through such an act can man survive.

Folk Songs in *The Grapes of Wrath*

H.R. Stoneback

In this excerpt from his article on the powerful influence of Steinbeck and folksinger Woodie Guthrie
on Americans' perception of the Okie experience,
H.R. Stoneback examines Steinbeck's use of folk
songs to suggest themes in the novel. In particular,
Stoneback focuses on the jukebox in chapter 16 and
the campfire scene in the following chapter to show
Steinbeck's juxtaposition of mechanical and heart-
felt music. The singing circle of chapter 17, Stoneback asserts, becomes an image of diverse people
coming together as one community. H.R. Stoneback
has taught at SUNY at New Paltz and is the author
of articles on Ernest Hemingway, William Faulkner,
Joseph Conrad, and others.

The work in which Steinbeck makes his most effective use of
folksong (and popular song) allusions is *The Grapes of Wrath.*
   The first words we hear from Jim Casy are in song—an
apt, memorable, and highly charged introduction to his
character—as he sings "in an easy thin tenor" what might
be called his "folksong" or "gospel" parody of the popular
hit song:

Yes, sir, that's my Saviour,
Je—sus is my Saviour,
Je—sus is my Saviour now.

   Throughout the novel, there are references to music—
e. g., the "glory-shoutin'" and gospel music of meetings, Tom
Joad's playing in a "strang band" in prison, the woman in the
camp whose soft voice soothes the child to sleep singing "Jesus loves you in the night," etc. But the two most important,
complex, and sustained treatments of song occur in Chapters Fifteen and Seventeen.

Reprinted from H.R. Stoneback, "'Rough People . . . Are the Best Singers': Woodie Guthrie,
John Steinbeck, and Folksong," in *The Steinbeck Question: New Essays in Criticism*, edited
by Donald R. Noble (Troy, NY: Whitson, 1993), by permission of the editor.

THE JUKEBOX

Chapter Fifteen begins with an evocation of a typical truck stop, a hamburger stand on Route 66, where the salient point of definition is the jukebox, "the nickel phonograph with records piled up like pies, ready to swing out to the turntable and play dance music, 'Ti-pi-ti-pi-tin,' 'Thanks for the Memory,' Bing Crosby, Benny Goodman." Steinbeck images a world of machines in a ruined "garden" through which people flee in cars that whiz "viciously" by on Route 66; he catalogues the machines, the cars and trucks on the road, and inside "this dump," inside Al's place, is another world of machines: slot machines, steaming coffee urns, chugging ice machines, humming electric fans, griddles hissing with hamburgers, and—the most significant "machine in the garden"—the jukebox. Two truck-drivers come in; one plays the slot machine, the other plays the jukebox and

> watches the disk slip free and the turntable rise up under it. Bing Crosby's voice—golden. "Thanks for the memory, of sunburn at the shore—You might have been a headache, but you never were a bore—" And the truck driver sings for Mae's ears, you might have been a haddock but you never was a whore—.

True to one of the oldest and most widespread folksong impulses, the truck-driver engages in bawdy song-parody, and releases into the folkloric stream of oral tradition another version of well-known song. (Did Steinbeck *invent* the "haddock" variation or hear it from someone else? It is a natural variation, one that seems remotely familiar to my ear, but since bawdy song-parodies are the least collected of all varieties of folksong, I can only suggest that this is probably one that Steinbeck heard somewhere. In any case, its appropriateness to the song and the situation is exact.) While the record plays, they talk, play the slot, tell jokes and laugh, apparently paying little attention to the song. Then, Steinbeck writes,

> Bing Crosby's voice stops. The turntable drops down and the record swings into its place in the pile. The purple light goes off. The nickel, which has caused all this mechanism to work, has caused Crosby to sing and an orchestra to play— this nickel drops from between the contact points into the box where the profits go. This nickel, unlike most money, has actually done a job of work, has been physically responsible for a reaction.

It is a detailed, closely focused description of the jukebox. And, to underline the point about machines and the world of mechanism, Steinbeck follows immediately with an image of the steam which "spurts from the valve of the coffee urn"; and the "compressor of the ice machine chugs softly" while the electric fan sweeps and "waves," and "the cars whiz by" outside. This is followed by the narration of the wreck, the big Cadillac hitting the overloaded "cut-down" car of a migrant family; then the 1926 Nash sedan pulls "wearily" into the truck-stop and some members of yet another dispossessed migrant family come in to get some bread. Machines, then, and especially the jukebox, receive an extraordinary emphasis in this chapter, and Steinbeck's imagistic tactics underline the careful strategy of juxtaposition with the next intercalary chapter.

CONTRASTING CHAPTERS

Chapter Seventeen, in contrast, focuses on a pre-machine world, a world that has little to do with "mechanism." Of course, the migrant families have cars to get them from one camp to the next, but these weary cars do not whiz "viciously," they creep, crawl, scuttle "like bugs to the westward." In the migrant camps, no hamburgers hiss on griddles, no coffee urns spurt, no ice machines chug, and there are no slot machines. They gather firewood, carry water, cook pork or sidemeat on the open fire; they boil bitter tea in a can; there is no ice but the migrants remember their old homes, the old cool spring-houses, the "little cool-house."

All of these contrasts function deliberately in Steinbeck's design, but the most striking juxtaposition in the paired chapters comes through the imagery of song. Once again, as in Chapter Fifteen, the core image of this chapter is song, and here it is the singing circle around the campfire, the human family "welded to one thing" through folksong; the living voices and the guitar—"a gracious thing"—are counterpoised against the mechanism of the jukebox and a detached, unheeded Bing Crosby singing "Thanks for the Memory." At first glance, it seems that Steinbeck has shaped these two chapters around the master motif of the machine-in-the-garden and the pre-mechanization pastoral idyll. Yet the design is far more subtle. In fact, both chapters are concerned with dispossession and community, with deracination [being forcibly moved from one's homeland] and memory. In

Chapter Seventeen the people in the camps retain their old home places in the telling, through the old tales and talking, through *memory* that is more than a mawkish attenuated echo from a jukebox, and they keep their hold on their lives, on their traditions, on their sense of community, through the singing of folksongs and gospel songs around the campfire. However diminished by the machine community may be, in whatever fashion "mechanism" displaces tradition, regardless of how trivial and sentimental Bing Crosby's mechanized voice crooning "Thanks for the Memory" may be when compared to the "eerie" laments and shared songs around the fire, the point of the paired scenes is that a sense of decency persists, a sense of human community lingers, *even* at the truck-stop. It may be on the way out, it may soon be no more than the sentimental "memory" of Crosby's song, but, still, amidst the hissing, whizzing, spurting, chugging, purple-lit machines, kindness lingers, as seen in the actions of Al and Mae and the truck-drivers. Yet, ultimately, the sense is that it may be a passing thing, that human community may find its final thin dry asseveration [declaration] by the vicious highway.

THE SINGING CIRCLE

Since Chapter Seventeen contains the most effective folksong scene or passage in all of Steinbeck's work, we should examine it in some detail here. At the beginning of the chapter Steinbeck writes of the "strange thing" that happens in the camps in the evenings, how "twenty families became one family," the "loss of home . . . one loss," and the "golden time in the West" one dream. As the guitar is the sacramental agent ministering to the dream and to memory, so are the songs—"all *of* the *people*" (emphasis added)—the binding element in the communion of the reconstituted larger family, the new community of the road, the migration. At the end of the chapter Steinbeck renders in detail a picking-and-singing session:

> And perhaps a man brought out his guitar . . . and everyone in the camp moved slowly in toward him. Many men can chord a guitar, but perhaps this man was a picker. There you have something—the deep chords beating, beating, while the melody runs on the strings like little footsteps.

A guitar-player might wish to see the actual picking rendered more felicitously, but Steinbeck's description leads effectively toward the main point, the singing circle image:

> The man played and the people moved slowly in on him un-
> til the circle was closed and tight, and then he sang "Ten-Cent
> Cotton and Forty-Cent Meat." And the circle sang softly with
> him. And he sang "Why Do You Cut Your Hair, Girls?" and the
> circle sang. He wailed the song, "I'm Leaving Old Texas," that
> eerie song that was sung before the Spaniards came, only the
> words were Indian then.

Speaking for the moment as a guitar-picker who has experienced the "singing circle" a thousand times, and as a writer
who knows the difficulty of rendering such numinous [spir-
itual] moments in time, I would assert that Steinbeck han-
dles the matter admirably. Yet, in order to gauge more exactly the effectiveness of this scene we should consider the
provenance and appropriateness of the songs to which
Steinbeck alludes, and the manner of presentation within
the overall scene. The choices open to a novelist rendering
such a singing scene are several: songs may simply be
named, as here, or a few key lines may be included in the
text, or the entire songs may be reproduced textually. Of the
choices, the latter is almost always ineffective, since it hin-
ders narrative and, more importantly, mixes modes, asks the
reader to hear a song that is in fact not present, since songs
do *not* exist—cannot be *present*—as a matter of text alone.
Still, as in some of the novels which most skillfully employ
folksong (such as William Faulkner's *Flags in the Dust* and
Elizabeth Madox Roberts' *The Time of Man*), a few evocative
lines of the song may well be included in the text, and this
would seem to be the best choice, better than the mere list of
titles which Steinbeck gives the reader. In fact, it is the business of allusion to arouse a curiosity that hungers for the
larger frame of reference, and these song-titles function as
allusions every bit as much as tags of poetry do in [T.S.
Eliot's poem] *The Waste Land*. Thus, since the songs mentioned (with the possible exception of "I'm Leaving Old
Texas") are not well-known, Steinbeck owes the reader a key
line or two, a core image from each song.

THE SONGS AND THEIR RELEVANCE

Having noted this as a minor flaw, however, I would insist
that Steinbeck has aptly *selected* the songs which carry the
scene. "Ten-Cent Cotton and Forty-Cent Meat" (also known
as "Seven-Cent Cotton and Forty-Cent Meat") is a country
blues song from the 1920s lamenting conditions for the cotton farmer, as in the first verse:

> Ten cent cotton and forty cent meat
> How in the world can a poor man eat?
> Flour up high, cotton down low,
> How in the world can we raise the dough?
> Clothes worn out, shoes run down,
> Old slouch hat with a hole in the crown;
> Back nearly broken and fingers all sore,
> Cotton gone down to rise no more.

The other verses continue in a similar vein, bemoaning the low prices the farmers get for everything they raise, and the high prices of everything they need to buy. The song is in the white country blues tradition of moderate protest, not in the radical left or Party-line or Popular Front tradition of protest songs which became predominant by c. 1940. That is to say, it is an exactly appropriate song for the people, the time, and the situation.

The next song that the circle sings, "Why Do You Cut Your Hair, Girls?", is a brush-arbor or camp-meeting song. Usually known as "Why Do You Bob Your Hair, Girls?", it was written in the 1920s and recorded by the West Virginia preacher Blind Alfred Reed (Victor 21350); it was a "hit" record and quickly entered oral tradition, especially in certain Fundamentalist circles, among the so-called "Holy Rollers." It is straightforwardly homiletic [preachy]:

> Why do you bob your hair, girls?
> You're doing mighty wrong;
> God gave it for a glory
> And you should wear it long.
> You spoil your lovely hair, girls,
> You keep yourself in style;
> Before you bob your hair, girls
> Just stop and think a while.

Subsequent verses insist that "short hair belongs to men," and warn that bobbing the hair is "breaking God's command"; the girls better not do it or they won't "reach the glory land." Again, the song is precisely right for the scene; it defines—if the reader *knows* the song—exactly who these *people* are; moreover, there is a certain resonance of California in that "glory land" which they may not "reach."

The third folksong is the "eerie" haunting old lament:

> I'm going to leave old Texas now
> They've got no use for the longhorn cow
> They've plowed and fenced my cattle range
> And the people now they're all so strange.

There are scores of versions and variants of this song in oral tradition and it is impossible to guess which version is sung in

Steinbeck's migrant camp; yet, since the constant emotional core of the song is deracination, dispossession from a loved place where new people have brought new strange ways, it is, once again, a precisely apt song for the migrant camps. I stress the aptness of the songs because it is very much to Steinbeck's credit that he avoids the pitfalls of other "union" novels of the 1930s, especially the worst kind of proletarian fiction that would have us believe, say, that the migrants in these camps sat around fires singing "Solidarity Forever," "Arise, You Workers," "The Internationale" [rallying song of revolutionary workers] or other so-called *Peoples* songs utterly inauthentic for the place and the people involved. The importance of song in *The Grapes of Wrath*, and the importance of having the *right* song is underlined, of course, by the title allusion as by Steinbeck's insistence to his publisher that the novel's endpapers print *"all all all* the verses of the Battle Hymn" as well as the music (Benson 387–88). It is to be noted that Steinbeck has nothing to say about the version of the "Battle Hymn"—much more frequently sung in 1930s leftist circles—known as "Solidarity Forever." In *The Grapes of Wrath*, then, we get the real songs of real people, made one in a singing circle:

> And now the group was welded to one thing, one unity, so that in the dark the eyes of the people were inward, and their minds played in other times, and their sadness was like rest, like sleep. He sang the "McAlester Blues" and then, to make up for it to the older people, he sang "Jesus Calls Me to His Side." The children drowsed with the music and went into the tents to sleep, and the singing came into their dreams.

PEOPLE UNITED IN SONG

This is *not* proletarian or *peoples* propaganda, but real folk singing. Finally, the guitar-picker is tired, and they all bid each other good night: "And each wished he could pick a guitar, because it is a gracious thing." Thus Steinbeck concludes one of the more effective scenes in the novel, one of the most challenging kinds of scene for a novelist to render. True folksong is here made to issue in the grace of community, a community of memory and desire, dispossession and destination. These "people," one feels, will be all right, and the image of their community lingers longer, for some readers at least, than any rhetoric about the "whole shebang," about the putative need to organize "One Big Solid Union." The entire scene is indeed "a gracious thing."

Biblical Imagery in *The Grapes of Wrath*

Leonard A. Slade Jr.

Leonard A. Slade Jr. analyzes the nature of the biblical imagery in *The Grapes of Wrath*. Slade neatly summarizes the parallels that many have noticed in the novel—how Casy and the Joads seem designed by Steinbeck to represent Jesus and his disciples, and how the novel describes a nearly biblical "exodus" from Oklahoma to a supposed land of milk and honey. Slade suggests that Casy's doctrine of love and spiritual unity is similar both to that of Jesus and to the transcendentalism of American philosopher Ralph Waldo Emerson. Leonard A. Slade Jr. has taught at Kentucky State University and the State University of New York at Albany. Among his books are *Another Black Voice: A Different Drummer* (1988), *The Beauty of Blackness* (1989), *I Fly Like a Bird* (1992), *The Whipping Song* (1993), *Vintage: New and Selected Poems* (1995), and *Fire Burning* (1995).

Biblical allusion is intrinsic to *The Grapes of Wrath*. The title of the novel, of course, refers to the line: "He is trampling out the vintage where the grapes of wrath are stored," in Julia Ward Howe's famous "Battle-Hymn of the Republic." The Hymn itself alludes to "the great wine press of the wrath of God," in Revelation. Apparently, then, the title suggests, moreover, "that the story exists in Christian context, indicating that we should expect to find some Christian meaning." Moreover, the symbol of grapes is used several times in the Bible to represent either wrath (as in Deuteronomy 32:32) or abundance (Numbers 13:12). Thus, many critics discuss Steinbeck's basic reference for his allegory: the exodus of the Hebrew People from Egypt, the land of Bondage, to the Promised Land of milk and honey. Too, the novel has three

Reprinted from Leonard A. Slade Jr., "The Use of Biblical Allusions in *The Grapes of Wrath*," *CLA Journal*, vol. 11, no. 3, March 1968, pp. 241–47, by permission of The College Language Association.

very clear divisions parallel to the Biblical story: Chapters 1 through 10 correspond to bondage in Egypt (where the bank and land companies fulfill the role of Pharaoh), and the plagues (drought and erosion); chapters 11 through 18 to the Exodus and journey through the wilderness (during which the old people die off); and chapters 19 through 30 to the settlement in the Promised Land—California, whose inhabitants are hostile, where false Gods hold sway, and where the migrants—like the children of Israel—formulate ethical codes (in the government camps). . . . The parallels (as will be shown) and mythic echoes are clear—even to Rose of Sharon's stillborn child floating down the river in an applebox, bringing to mind the story of Moses, although here it is the mother rather than the child who represents hope. . . .

JIM CASY AS JESUS CHRIST

One critic thinks that the Joad philosophy—that which Casy preaches—has "stronger, more direct relations to the Bible" than the relationship of the Joad philosophy to the transcendentalism of Emerson and Whitman. Then, too, there seems to be a "Christ-Casy relationship." More specifically, [Martin] Shockley states, Jesus commenced his mission after He came out of the wilderness, where He meditated; "Preacher Casy comes into the book after a similar treatment." He tells Tom, " 'Nobody seen me. I went off alone, an' I sat and figured. The sperit's strong in me, on'y it ain't the same.' " It is later in the book when Tom and Casy meet in the strikers' tent; Casy says he has " 'been a-goin' into the wilderness like Jesus to find out somepin.' " Steinbeck seems conscious of the parallel. Shockley states:

> Like Jesus, Jim has rejected an old religion and is in process of replacing it with a new gospel. In the introductory scene with Tom Joad, Tom and Jim recall the old days when Casy preached the old religion, expounded the old concept of sin and guilt. Now, however, Casy explains his rejection of a religion through which he saw himself as wicked and depraved because of the satisfaction of natural human desires. The old Adam of the fall is about to be exorcised through the new dispensation.

Jim Casy can be identified simply and directly with Christ, and his words paraphrase the words of Jesus, who said, " 'God is love' " and " 'A new commandment I give unto you: that ye love one another.' " Casy's voice rang, " 'What's this call, this sperit? It's love. I love people so much I'm fit to bust, sometimes.' " This seems to be the truth Casy has found in his wilderness, the gospel he brings back to the people he loves.

Finally, Casy's death symbolically occurs in the middle of a stream to represent the "crossing over Jordan" Christian motif. Particularly significant, however, are Casy's last words directed to the man who murders him. "'Listen,'" he said. "'You fellas don' know what you're doin.'" Casy repeats this a second time. Jesus said, as they crucified Him, "'Father, forgive them; for they know not what they do.'" Then it is not long before Tom becomes Casy's disciple. He has learned from his master, and now takes up his master's work. Two of Jesus' disciples were named Thomas. Most of those chosen by Him to found the religion we profess were called from among people like the Joads. Thus, Shockley sees "evidence of a Christ-Casy relationship," and "Jim Casy unmistakably and significantly equates with Jesus Christ." Accordingly, in *The Grapes of Wrath* there is "a sequence of familiar Christian symbols, appearing at structural crises of the plot, dominating the narrative, determining the characterization, revealing the theme as conscious and consistent Christian allegory."

Exodus from Oklahoma

More interpretations have been made of the mythical side and of other Biblical parallels. "The name *Joad*," [Joseph] Fontenrose suggests, " is meant to suggest *Judah*." The Joads had lived in Oklahoma peacefully since the first settlement; as the Hebrews had lived in Egypt since Joseph's time. But there arose a new king over Egypt, who did not know Joseph." And the monster, representing a changed economic order, and quite as hard-hearted as Pharaoh, knew not the Joads and their kin. In Oklahoma the dust filtered into every house and settled on everything, as in one of the Egyptian plagues the dust became lice which settled on man and beast. The Bible reads:

> And they did so; Aaron stretched out his hand with his rod, and struck the dust of the earth, and there came gnats of man and beast; all the dust of the earth became gnats throughout all the land of Egypt.

Furthermore, the dust ruined the corn, as hail ruined the Egyptians' flax and barley, and it made the night as black as the plague of darkness in Egypt. On the eve of departure the Joads slaughtered two pigs, more likely victims in Oklahoma that the lambs sacrificed by the Hebrews on Passover. But whereas the Hebrews despoiled the Egyptians of jewels before leaving, "the Joads and other Okies were despoiled of goods and money by sharp businessmen in the land that they left."

On the road west the Joads met men who were going back to Oklahoma from California. These men reported that although California was a lovely and rich country the residents were hostile to the migrant workers, treated them badly, and paid them so poorly that many migrants starved to death in slack periods. Scouts whom Moses, in the Bible, sent ahead into Canaan came back with the report that " it flows with milk and honey"; but the natives of that land were giants who looked upon the Hebrews as locusts. The Bible reads:

> So they brought to the people of Israel an evil report of the land which they had spied out, saying, "The land, through which we have gone, to spy it out, is a land that devours its inhabitants; and all the people that we saw in it are men of great stature."

Yet the Joads, like Joshua and Caleb, were determined to enter the land. The cruelty of California officers at the border, the efforts to turn back indigent migrants, the refusal of cities and towns to let migrant workers enter, except when their labor was needed—in all this we may see the efforts of the Edomites, Moabites, and Amonites to keep the Israelites from entering their countries.

THE NEW MOSES

There is, also, a most striking episodic parallel to Exodus near the end of the novel. When Tom killed the vigilante who struck Casy down and left the region when it seemed that he would be found out, he acted as Moses had done. When Moses grew up, according to the Bible, he saw an Egyptian beating a Hebrew laborer, and he killed the Egyptian and hid his body in the sand. The next day when he reproved a Hebrew for striking another, the angry offender said that he intended to kill him just as he had killed the Egyptian. Then Moses left Pharaoh and went to Midian. "In the Pentateuch [the first five books of the Old Testament] this happened in Egypt before the Exodus; in *The Grapes of Wrath* it happened in California after the migration." The "house of bondage" is in the new land; in the old land the people had lived in patriarchal contentment until they were forced to leave. It seems to be similar to Israel's earlier migration from Palestine to Egypt. Just after reaching California, Tom told Casy that it was not a land of milk and honey like the preachers said. Moses has found out that "his task of delivering his people from bondage is just beginning, not ending; it is now that he strikes the first blow. The migrants have gained nothing by merely exchanging one land for another; they must deal with the 'mean thing.'" Thus, Tom Joad becomes the new Moses who will lead the oppressed people, succeeding Jim Casy, who had found One Big Soul in the hills, as Moses had found the Lord on Mount Horeb [another name for Mount Sinai].

CASEY AND THE TWELVE DISCIPLES

Fontenrose thinks, unlike a few critics, that "the correspondences between the gospel story and Steinbeck's novel go" deep. Specifically, thirteen persons started west, Casy and twelve Joads, who, as has been said, also represent Judea, where Jesus came to teach. Two of the Joads were named Thomas, and another one was named John; then, too, Casy's name was James, brother and disciple of Jesus. One of the twelve, Connie Rivers, was not really a Joad; he is Judas, for not only did he desert the Joads selfishly at a critical moment, but just before he did so he told his wife that he would have done better "'if he stayed home an' studied up tractors.'" The tractor driver of Chapter Five got three dollars a day. Interestingly, three dollars are thirty pieces of silver. Further, there is the crowing of roosters on the night when Casy was killed. Steinbeck writes that "at last the roosters crowed, far away, and gradually the window lightened. The dawn came finally." This happens at a time when the Joads had to deny Tom.

Equally important, Casy taught a doctrine that "coincided in certain respects with Jesus' doctrine: love for all men, sympathy for the poor and oppressed, realization of the gospel in active ministry, subordination of formal observances to men's real needs and of property to humanity, and toleration of men's weaknesses and sensual desires." Moreover, after worrying about his sexual backsliding, Casy came to the conclusion that

> Maybe it ain't a sin. Maybe it's just the way folks is. . . . There ain't no sin and there ain't no virtue. There's just stuff people do. It's all part of the same thing. And some of the things folks do is nice, and some ain't nice, but that's as far as any man got a right to say.

THE UNITY OF MANKIND

It seems that Casy's doctrine of sin led to his positive doctrine of love: "'. . . maybe it's all men an' all women we love; maybe that's the Holy Sperit—the human sperit—the whole shebang. Maybe all men gote one big soul ever' body's a part of." And so he arrived at the doctrine of the Oversoul. In a California jail, however, his doctrine took complete shape as a social gospel, and Casy's ministry became the organizing of farm workers into unions.

Fontenrose concludes that "in no Steinbeck novel do the . . . mythical strands fit so neatly together as in *The Grapes of Wrath.*" The Oklahoma land company is at once monster, Leviathan [a large, biblical sea animal], and Pharoah oppressing the tenant farmers, who are equally monster's prey and Israelites. It is also believed that

> The California land companies are Canaanites, Pharisees, Roman government, and the dominant organism of an ecological community. The [f]amily organisms are forced to join together into a larger collective organism; the Hebrews' migration and sufferings weld them into a united nation; the poor and oppressed receive a Messiah who teaches them unity in the Oversoul. The Joads are equally a family unit, the twelve tribes of Israel, and the twelve disciples. Casy and Tom are both Moses and Jesus as leaders of the people and guiding organs in the new collective organism.

Thus, that which is mythical builds up to a single conclusion: the unity of all mankind. . . .

In summary and conclusion, there seems to be a universal pattern which repeats itself in *The Grapes of Wrath*: a pattern of dispossession; of nobility achieved by sacrifice necessitated by suffering; of wandering in the wilderness of exile; of struggle, defeat, hope, and eventual victory; of decadence and renewed struggles—here is an allegory of humanity itself. And it is in this sense, I think, that the Joads are indeed the Old Testament Jews, just as the Jews might be considered the Biblical Joads: the poor people exiled from bondage which was their home for many generations; suffering exile; descending upon the "Land of Milk and Honey" much to the horror of those who had already settled in the Promised Land; and finding strength in their strange Gods (that is, the "new religion" of Casy the ex-preacher), in a ferocity of will-to-survive and in a sense of outraged human dignity. In addition, Steinbeck has made the Joads representative of the American pioneer and, by investing them and their story with Biblical elements, has made their characters more universal than they could have otherwise been. As has been pointed out, as one example, the use of Jim Casy as a Christ-figure plainly reveals the author's intent. Like Stephen Crane with Jim Conklin in *The Red Badge of Courage*, Steinbeck obviously attempted to show the parallel by giving him the same initials (i.e., J.C. for Jesus Christ). Also, the vocabulary, rhythm, imagery, and tone are pronounced similarities to the language of the Bible. Such similarities may be seen in qualities of simplicity, purity, strength, vigor, and earnestness. The novel, in addition, contains passages of prophetic power, not only in dialogue, but even in descriptive and expository passages. Finally, then, Steinbeck is attempting to illuminate for his readers universal rather than particular struggles. And it is at this point that Steinbeck's Biblical analogy and parallels combine with a concept of the nature of human conflicts.

Machines and Animals in *The Grapes of Wrath*

Robert J. Griffin and William A. Freedman

Robert J. Griffin and William A. Freedman's often-anthologized essay provides an overview of the images of animals and machines that are everywhere in Steinbeck's long narrative. Their very pervasiveness suggests their importance to Steinbeck. Despite potential negative connotations associated with both motifs, Steinbeck is not antimachine, nor does he believe that the Okies are to be equated with animals. Instead, Griffin and Freedman point out how Steinbeck uses these two major patterns of imagery to connect interchapters with chapters, to play important roles in the literal story, to underscore themes, and to give the novel unity. Robert J. Griffin has taught at Yale and the University of California at Berkeley. William A. Freedman has taught at the University of Chicago and Haifa University in Israel. Both are widely published authors of studies on English and American literature.

In this paper we should like to concentrate on two pervasive motifs in the novel, namely, the crucially important motifs of *machines* and *animals* which contribute considerably to structure and thematic content. We may call these two the "dominant motifs," but we must remember that extracting these elements is necessarily an act of oversimplification; it is only through their complex relationships with subsidiary motifs and devices, and with the more straightforward narration and exposition and argumentation, that they provide major symbols integral to the art and substance of the novel. With this qualification in mind, we may proceed to a consideration of machines and animals as sources of tropes, as signs and underscoring devices, and ultimately as persistent symbols.

Adapted from Robert J. Griffin and William A. Freedman, "Machines and Animals: Pervasive Motifs in *The Grapes of Wrath*," *Journal of English and Germanic Philology*, vol. 67, no. 3, July 1963, pp. 569–80. Copyright 1963 by the Board of Trustees of the University of Illinois. Used with the permission of the University of Illinois Press.

STEINBECK RARELY USES MACHINES METAPHORICALLY

Very few of the tropes of the novel—the metaphors, similes, and allusions—make use of machinery as such. "Tractored out" is of course a prominent figure of speech repeated several times to express the Okies' plight in being forced from their plots of land by the mechanical monstrosity of industrialized farming ("tractored off" also appears a couple of times). But otherwise about the only instance of a metaphorical use of machinery is a single simile late in the novel: the weary men trying to build a bank of earth to hold back the flood "worked jerkily, like machines." There are a good many metaphors applied to mechanical apparatuses—that is, tropes in which machinery is characterized by some non-mechanical phenomenon as the vehicle of the metaphor. Generally this metaphorical characterization of machines emphasizes animalism or the bestial side of human affairs, as the seeders are said to rape the land. Fundamentally these metaphors appear designed to contribute to a general sense of tragedy or disaster indicated by such secondary motifs as the blood tropes—"the sun was as red as ripe new blood," "the earth was bloody in [the sun's] setting light,"—and the frequent recurrence of "cut"—"the sun cut into the shade," "the road was cut with furrows."

ANIMAL METAPHORS ABOUND

While there are very few machine tropes, animal tropes abound. Often animals are used to characterize the human sex drive: Muley Graves (whose name is not inappropriate here) refers to himself during his first experience as "snortin' like a buck deer, randy as a billygoat"; young, virile Al Joad has been "a-billygoatin' aroun' the country. Tomcattin' hisself to death." And the sexuality of animals several times appears as the vehicle of a metaphor: Casy refers to a participant in a revival meeting as "jumpy as a stud horse in a box stall." Animal tropes frequently serve to denote violence or depravity in human behavior: fighting "like a couple of cats"; a tractor hitting a share-cropper's cabin "give her a shake like a dog shakes a rat"; Muley used to be "mean like a wolf" but now is "mean like a weasel"; and Ma Joad describes Purty Boy Floyd's career as comparable to a maddened animal at bay—"they shot at him like a varmint, an' he shot back, an' then they run him like a coyote, an' him a-snappin' an' a-snarlin', mean as a lobo." Animal tropes may simply indicate a harmless playfulness or swagger: Winfield Joad is "kid-wild and calfish," and Al acts like "a dung-hill rooster." But the most frequent and significant use of the numerous animal tropes is to characterize the Okies' plight: the Joads are forced off their forty acres, forced to live "piled in John's house like gophers in a winter burrow"; then they begin an abortive trip toward what they hope will prove to be a "New Canaan" in California, and Casy uses this tacit analogy to describe the impersonal, industrial economy from which they are fleeing:

> Ever see one a them Gila monsters take hold, mister? Grabs hold, an' you chop him in two an' his head hangs on. Chop him at the neck an' his head hangs on. Got to take a screwdriver an' pry his head apart to git him loose. An' while he's layin' there, poison is drippin' an' drippin' into the hole he's made with his teeth.

Casy argues that the wrong results from men not staying "harnessed" together in a common effort ("mankin' was holy when it was one thing"); one man can get "the bit in his teeth an' run off his own way, kickin' an' draggin' an' fightin'." Consequently the roads to California are "full of frantic people running like ants." In California the Okies work, when they can get work, "like draft horses"; they are driven "like pigs" and forced to live "like pigs." Casy has been observing and listening to the Okies in their misfortunes, and he knows their fear and dissatisfaction and restlessness: "I hear 'em an' feel 'em; an' they're beating their wings like a bird in a attic. Gonna bust their wings on a dusty winda tryin' ta get out."

It should be noted that the animalistic references to people are not as a rule unfavorable ("randy as a billygoat" is scarcely a pejorative in Steinbeck's lusty lexicon). The few derogatory animal tropes are almost all applied to the exploiters (banks, land companies, profiteers) and not to the exploited (the Joads and other Okies). That these latter must behave like the lower animals is not their fault. Their animalism is the result of the encroachments of the machine economy. Machines, then, are frequently depicted as evil objects: they "tear in and shove the croppers out"; "one man on a tractor can take the place of twelve or fourteen families"; so the Okies must take to the road, seeking a new home, lamenting, "I lost my land, a single tractor took my land."

Farming has become a mechanized industry, and Steinbeck devotes an entire chapter (nineteen) to the tragic results:

> The tractors which throw men out of work, the belt lines which carry loads, the machines which produce, all were increased; and more and more families scampered on the highways, looking for crumbs from the great holdings, lusting after the land beside the roads. The great owners formed associations for protection and they met to discuss ways to intimidate, to kill, to gas.

The Okies are very aware of the evils brought about by mechanization. Reduced to picking cotton for bare-subsistence wages, they realize that even this source of income may soon go. One asks, "Heard 'bout the new cotton-pickin' machine?"

AN AGE OF MACHINERY

The Joads find themselves living—trying to live—in an age of machinery. Machines or mechanized devices quite naturally play important roles in the symbolism of the novel. ("Symbolism" is here understood to mean the employment of concrete images—objects and events—to embody or suggest abstract qualities or concepts.) Some machines serve as "interior" symbols; they are, that is, recognized as symbolic by characters in the novel. Still others, largely because of the frequency with which or crucial contexts in which they appear, can be seen by the careful reader to take on symbolic significance. The "huge red transport truck" of chapter two, for example, can be seen as a sort of epitome of the mechanical-industrial economy—the bigness, the newness, the mobility, the massive efficiency, even the inhumanity (*No Riders*) and lack of trust—"a brass padlock stood straight out from the hasp on the big back doors." It is a mobile era in which one must accommodate to the mass mechanization in order to survive. Farmers can no longer hope to get by with a team and a wagon. And Steinbeck finds in the used-car business (chapter seven), preying on the need to move out and move quickly, an apt representation for the exploitation of those who have not yet been able to accommodate: "In the towns, on the edges of the towns, in fields, in vacant lots, the used-car yards, the wreckers' yards, the garages with blazoned signs—Used Cars, Good Used Cars, Cheap transportation." The Joads' makeshift truck aptly represents their predicament—their need to move, their inability to move efficiently or in style, their over-all precariousness: "The engine was noisy, full of little clashings, and the brake rods banged. There was a wooden creaking from the wheels, and a thin jet of steam escaped through a hole in the top of the radiator cap." Steinbeck makes overt the symbolic nature of this truck; when the members of the family meet for their final council before migrating, they meet near the truck: "The house was dead, and the fields were dead; but this truck was the active thing, the living principle." Here, as throughout the novel, the Joads' predicament is a representative instance of the predicaments of thousands. Highway 66 is the "main migrant road" (chapter twelve), and on this "long concrete path" move the dispossessed, the "people in flight": "In the day ancient leaky radiators sent up columns of steam, loose connecting rods hammered and pounded. And the men driving the trucks and the overloaded cars listened apprehensively. How far between towns? It is a terror between towns. If something breaks—well, if something breaks we camp right here while Jim walks to town and gets a part and walks back." Along this route the dispossessed farmers find that they are not alone in their troubles. The independent, small-scale service station operator is being squeezed out of his livelihood just as the farmers have been; Tom tells the poor operator that he too will soon be a part of the vast moving. And the various types of vehicles moving along Route 66 are obvious status symbols. Some have "class an' speed"; these are the insolent chariots of the exploiters. Others are the beat-up, overloaded conveyors of the exploited in search of a better life. The reactions of those who are better-off to the sad vehicles of the Okies are representative of their lack of understanding and sympathy:

"Jesus, I'd hate to start out in a jalopy like that."
"Well, you and me got sense. Them goddamn Okies got no sense and no feeling. They ain't human. A human being wouldn't live like they do. A human being couldn't stand it to be so dirty and miserable. They ain't a hell of a lot better than gorillas."

The Okies are conscious of vehicles as status symbols and automatically distrust anyone in a better car. When a new Chevrolet pulls into the laborers' camp, the laborers automatically know that it brings trouble. Similarly the condition of the Okies' vehicles provides perfect parallels for their own sad state. As the Joads are trying to move ahead without being able to ascertain exactly where they are headed—"even if we got to crawl"—so their truck's "dim lights felt along the broad black highway ahead." As the Joads' condition worsens, so naturally does that of their truck (e.g., "the right head light blinked on and off from a bad connection"). In the development of the novel their vehicles are so closely identified with the Okies that a statement of some damage to the vehicles becomes obviously symbolic of other troubles for the owners. When the disastrous rains come, "beside the tents the old cars stood, and water fouled the ignition wires and water fouled the carburetors." The disastrousness of the ensuing flood is quite clearly signaled by mention of the "trucks and automobiles deep in the slowly moving water."

CASY AND THE TURTLE

Steinbeck's symbolic turtle in chapter three is most significantly associated with Jim Casy. Critic Joyce Compton Brown argues that Steinbeck matches the turtle's physical characteristics with Casy, a lone wanderer who becomes a reluctant voice of the people.

The strongest connection between the turtle and the people comes through Casy, who exhibits turtle-like traits. He observes the turtle and comments, "Nobody can't keep a turtle though. They work at it and work at it, and at last one day they get out and away they go—off somewheres." Not only has Casy been "off somewheres" meditating, he is destined to go across the country in the direction that the turtle is heading—southwest. And nobody can keep Casy; he soon leaves the Joads to go his own direction. Like the turtle, which is shy by nature, Casy too is shy, no longer willing to function as preacher. When asked to say grace, he protests; when he asks to go with the Joads, he is "embarrassed by his own speech." When Grampa is dying, Granma orders Casy to pray, but he replies, "I can't. . . ." Only when Granma screams, "Pray, goddam you," will Casy consent to pray; even then he merely repeats part of the Lord's Prayer. To avoid being asked to pray at Grampa's funeral, he walks away while Tom comments, "He don't like to pray no more." Even when Sairy Wilson, dying, asks him to pray, he hesitates, agreeing only to a silent prayer to no God in particular.

More significant is Steinbeck's use of descriptive phrases suggesting a turtle-like appearance in the depiction of Casy's head:

THE OKIES' PETS AS SYMBOLS

As the Okies' vehicles provide an accurate index to their circumstances, so do the animals they own, particularly their pets. The deserted cat that Tom and Casy find when they survey the Joads' deserted farm represents the forlorn state of the dispossessed (the cat actually foreshadows the appearance of Muley Graves with his tales of lonely scavengering). The dogs that appear when Tom and Casy reach Uncle John's place are indicative of human behavior in the face of new circumstances (one sniffs cautiously up to examine the strangers, while the other seeks some adequate excuse for avoiding the possible danger). After the company's tractors move in and the share-croppers are "shoved

It was a long head, bony, tight of skin, and set on a neck as stringy and muscular as a celery stalk. His eyeballs were heavy and protruding; the lids stretched to cover them, and the lids were raw and red. His cheeks were brown and shiny and hairless and his mouth full—humorous or sensual. The nose, beaked and hard, stretched the skin so tightly that the bridge showed white. There was no perspiration on the face, not even on the tall pale forehead.

The description is amazingly applicable to the box turtle. Casy shows the reptilian characteristic of not perspiring on a day so hot that Tom Joad "mopped his wet face." The box turtle is brown as are Casy's cheeks and, like Casy, it has a large mouth. It appears to have a "nose," a ridge which is tightly covered with skin and which, like Casy's, resembles a beak. The eyes are normally brown, but in the male are sometimes red. Casy's eyes are brown but red-rimmed. The eyes of the turtle have yellow specks in them comparable to Casy's "golden specks." Certainly all turtles have long bony heads barely distinguishable from their muscular necks. Steinbeck further points out that Casy's skin is "shiny and hairless" like that of the turtle. While the reference to Casy's "great horse teeth" may appear to be unrelated to the turtle imagery, the box turtle does have horny plates which serve as teeth and are a part of its mouth. Steinbeck also suggests the analogy by reference to the "horny beak" of the turtle, its "front clawed feet" and "hands," and Casy's "bony hand."

The turtle imagery . . . assist in conveying allegorically the concept of Casy as the lonely wanderer who serves as the reluctant voice of the people.

Joyce Compton Brown, "Steinbeck's The Grapes of Wrath," *Explicator*, vol. 41, no. 4, Summer 1983, pp. 50–51.

off" their land, the pets that they left behind must fend for themselves and thus gradually revert to the primitive state of their ancestors—a reversion not unlike the desperate measures that the Okies are driven to by adversity and animosity: "The wild cats crept in from the fields at night, but they did not mew at the doorstep any more. They moved like shadows of a cloud across the moon, into the rooms to hunt the mice." The Joads take a dog with them on their flight to California, but he is not prepared to adjust to the new, fast, mechanized life thrust upon him; when his owners stop for gas and water, he wanders out to the great highway—"A big swift car whisked near, tires squealed. The dog dodged helplessly, and with a shriek, cut off in the middle, went under the wheels." The owner of the dilapidated independent service station comments on the sad scene, "A dog jus' don' last no time near a highway. I had three dogs run over in a year. Don't keep none, no more." After the Joads have been in California for a while and discover the grim facts of life for them there, they move on to another "Hooverville" camp of migrants. They find their fellow job-seekers hungry, fearful, and distrustful; the single pet there vividly expresses the general attitude or atmosphere of the place: "A lean brown mongrel dog came sniffing around the side of the tent. He was nervous and flexed to run. He sniffed close before he was aware of the two men, and then looking up he saw them, leaped sideways, and fled, ears back, bony tail clamped protectively." Yet having pets is indicative of the love and sympathy of which man is capable when in favorable circumstances. The simple, "natural" Joads never lose their appreciation for pets. When their fortunes are at their lowest ebb, Ma still holds hopes for a pleasant future: "'Wisht we had a dog,' Ruthie said. [Ma replied] 'We'll have a dog; have a cat too.'"

STEINBECK'S USE OF EPITOME

Pets, then, serve as symbolic indices to human situations; and other animal symbols are used to excellent advantage. One of Steinbeck's favorite devices is the use of epitome—the description of some object or event, apart from the main movement of the narrative, which symbolically sums up something central to the meaning of the narrative. Toward the end of *The Grapes of Wrath* the migrants are gathered about a fire, telling stories, and one of them recounts an experience of a single Indian brave whom they were forced to shoot—epitomizing the indomitability and dignity of man, and foreshadowing Casy's fate.

THE TURTLE

We have already noted the use of animals for symbolic foreshadowing (for instance, the dispossessed cat and Muley Graves). Probably Steinbeck's most famous use of the symbolic epitome is the land turtle. The progress of the Okies, representative of the perseverance of "Manself," is neatly foreshadowed in the description of the turtle's persistent forward movement: he slowly plods his way, seeking to prevail in the face of adversities, and he succeeds in spite of insects, such obstacles as the highway, motorists' swerving to hit him (though some swerve to avoid hitting him), Tom's imprisoning him for awhile in his coat, the attacks of a cat, and so on. Steinbeck does not leave discernment of the rich parallels wholly to the reader's imagination. There are, for instance, similarities between Tom's progress along the dirt road and the turtle's: "And as the turtle crawled on down the embankment, its shell dragged dirt over the seeds . . . drawing a wavy shallow trench in the dust with its shell"; and "Joad plodded along, dragging his cloud of dust behind him . . . dragging his heels a little in the dust" (at this point in the novel Tom has not yet begun to sow the seeds of new growth among the downtrodden Okies). Casy remarks on the indomitability of the turtle, and its similarity to himself: "Nobody can't keep a turtle though. They work at it and work at it, and at last one day they get out and away they go—off somewheres. It's like me." But at this point in the novel Casy is not altogether like the turtle, for he has not yet discovered the goal to which he will devote himself unstintingly: "'Goin' someplace,' he repeated. 'That's right, he's goin' someplace. Me—I don't know where I'm goin'.'"

Animal epitomes, such as the turtle and the "lean gray cat," occur several times at crucial points. And frequently a person's character will be represented by his reaction to or treatment of lower animals. As Tom and Casy walk along the dusty road a gopher snake wriggles across their path; Tom peers at it, sees that it is harmless, and says, " 'Let him go.'" Tom is not cruel or vicious, but he does recognize the need to prevent or put down impending disaster. Later, a "rattlesnake crawled across the road and Tom hit it and broke it and left it squirming." The exploitation of the Okies is symbolized by the grossly unfair price paid a share-cropper for the matched pair of bay horses he is forced to sell. In this purchase of the bays, the exploiters are buying a part of the croppers' history, their loves and labors; and a swelling bitterness is part of the bargain: "You're buying years of work, toil in the sun; you're buying a sorrow that can't talk. But watch it, mister."

Animals convey symbolic significance throughout the novel. When the Okies are about to set out on what they are aware will be no pleasure jaunt to California—though they scarcely have any idea how dire will be the journey and the life at the end of it—an ominous "shadow of a buzzard slid across the earth, and the family all looked up at the sailing black bird." In the light of the more obvious uses of animals as epitomes or omens, it is easy to see that other references to animals, which might otherwise seem incidental, are intentionally parallel to the actions or troubles of people. Here is a vivid parallel for the plight of the share-cropper, caught in the vast, rapid, mechanized movement of the industrial economy (the great highway is persistently the bearer of symbolic phenomena):

> A jackrabbit got caught in the lights and he bounced along ahead, cruising easily, his great ears flopping with every jump. Now and then he tried to break off the road, but the wall of darkness thrust him back. Far ahead bright headlights appeared and bore down on them. The rabbit hesitated, faltered, then turned and bolted toward the lesser lights of the Dodge. There was a small soft jolt as he went under the wheels. The oncoming car swished by.

As the weary Okies gather in a Hooverville to try to find some way out of the disaster they have flown into, moths circle frantically about the single light: "A lamp bug slammed into the lantern and broke itself, and fell into darkness." While the wary mongrel at the camp represents the timorous doubts of the Okies, the arrogant skunks that prowl about at night are reminiscent of the imperious deputies and owners who intimidate the campers. The Okies are driven like animals, forced to live like animals, and frequently the treatment they receive from their short-term employers is not as good as that given farm animals:

> Fella had a team of horses, had to use 'em to plow an' cultivate an' mow, wouldn' think a turnin' 'em out to starve when they wasn't workin'.
>
> Them's horses—we're men.

. . . We have seen that machines are usually instruments or indices of misfortune in Steinbeck's novel. But to assume that machinery is automatically or necessarily bad for Steinbeck would be a serious mistake. Machines are *instruments*, and in the hands of the right people they can be instruments of good fortune. When the turtle tries to cross the highway, one driver tries to smash him, while another swerves to miss him; it depends on who is behind the wheel. Al's relationship with the truck is indicative of the complex problems of accommodating in a machine age. He knows about motors, so he can take care of the truck and put it to good use. He is admitted to a place of responsibility in the family council because of his up-to-date ability. He becomes "the soul of the car." The young people are more in tune with the machines of their times, whereas the older ones are not prepared to accommodate to the exigencies of the industrial economy:

> Casy turned to Tom. "Funny how you fellas can fix a car. Jus' light right in an' fix her. I couldn't fix no car, not even now when I seen you do it."
>
> "Got to grow into her when you're a little kid," Tom said. "It ain't jus' knowin'. It's more'n that. Kids now can tear down a car 'thout even thinkin' about it."

The tractors that shove the croppers off their land are not inherently evil; they are simply the symptoms of unfair exploitation. In one of the interchapters (fourteen) Steinbeck expresses the thought that the machines are in themselves of neutral value:

> Is a tractor bad? Is the power that turns the long furrows wrong? If this tractor were ours it would be good—not mine, but ours. If our tractor turned the long furrows of our land, it would be good. Not my land, but ours. We could love that tractor then as we have loved this land when it was ours. But this tractor does two things—it turns the land and turns us off the land. There is little difference between this tractor and a tank. The people are driven, intimidated, hurt by both.

Machinery, like the science and technology that can develop bigger and better crops, is not enough for progress; there must be human understanding and cooperation. The Okies— through a fault not really their own—have been unable to adjust to the machinery of industrialization. Toward the very last of the novel Ma pleads with Al not to desert the family, because he is the only one left qualified to handle the truck that has become so necessary a part of their lives. As the flood creeps up about the Joads, the truck is inundated, put out of action. But the novel ends on a hopeful note of human sharing, and we may surmise that the Okies (or at least their children) can eventually assimilate themselves into a machine-oriented society. . . .

The animal motif in *Grapes* does not at all indicate that man is or ought to be exactly like the lower animals. The Okies crawl across the country like ants, live like pigs, and fight amongst themselves like cats, mainly because they have been forced into this animalistic existence. Man can plod on in his progress like the turtle, but he can also become conscious of his goals and deliberately employ new devices in attaining those goals. Man's progress need not be blind; for he can couple human knowledge with human love, and manipulate science and technology to make possible the betterment of himself and all his fellows. Steinbeck does not present a picture of utopia in his novel, but the dominant motifs do indicate that such a society is possible.

STEINBECK'S MASTERFUL MANIPULATION OF IMAGERY

It has been a fundamental assumption of this study that dominant motifs are of central importance in the form and meaning of certain works of fiction. In this particular case we would contend that Steinbeck's intricate and masterful manipulation of the various references to machines and animals is an essential factor in the stature of *The Grapes of Wrath* as one of the monuments of twentieth-century American literature. By their very pervasiveness—the recurrence of the components that constitute the motifs—the references contribute significantly to the unity of the work; they help, for instance, to bind together the Joad chapters with those which generalize the meaning that the Joads' story illustrates. Certain animals and machines play important parts on the literal level of the story, and these and others serve to underscore principal developments or "themes" in the novel. Certain animals and machines are recognizably symbolic within the context of the story, and still others (the epitomes for example) can be discerned as much more meaningful than their overt, apparently incidental mention might at first seem to indicate. Both the interior and the more subtle symbols—as reinforced by the recurrence of related allusions or figures of speech—are interwoven and played off against one another to such an extent that the over-all meaning is not merely made more vivid: it is considerably enriched.

CHAPTER 4

Reception and Continuing Relevance

Steinbeck Speaks for All Immigrants

Mimi Reisel Gladstein

Mimi Reisel Gladstein, professor of English at the
University of Texas in El Paso, is well known for her
feminist perspectives on Steinbeck's women. Here
she defends *The Grapes of Wrath* as an important
study of the immigrant experience. The Joads's
struggle, she writes, is a powerful representation of
the universal struggle of immigrants to achieve "the
dream". Immigrants all over the world have faced
this struggle, met with similar setbacks, and fought
hard to overcome stereotyping and prejudice.

The many conferences and publications honoring the fifti-
eth anniversary of *The Grapes of Wrath* in 1989 give strong
indication of the durability of John Steinbeck's world-
famous novel. There are still a few holdouts such as Leslie
Fiedler, who fudges his condemnation of this "problematic
middlebrow book" by allowing the "ambiguous, archetypal
final scene" to "redeem" the work, but even hardened
Steinbeck-basher Harold Bloom concedes that "no canonical
standards worthy of human respect could exclude *The
Grapes of Wrath* from a serious reader's esteem." And while
expressing his reservations, Bloom is still "grateful for the
novel's continued existence."

If further assurance is needed, and I think it is not, of the
book's continued and continuing significance, the success of
the Steppenwolf Theatre Company production of *The Grapes
of Wrath* in Chicago, La Jolla, London, and on Broadway
adds evidence of the ability of the story to capture new audiences. Frank Galati's adaptation of Steinbeck's novel has
elicited a chorus of praise from critics, each with his or her
own explanation of the reason why Steinbeck's timely tale of
a problem in the 1930s continues to engage us in the 1990s.

Reprinted from Mimi Reisel Gladstein, "*The Grapes of Wrath:* Steinbeck and the Eternal Immigrant," in *John Steinbeck: The Years of Greatness, 1936–1939*, edited by Tetsumaro Hayashi, by permission of the publisher. Copyright © 1993 by The University
of Alabama Press.

To this end, the *USA Today* article about the production was headlined "New *Grapes* Still Bears Fruit." Terry Kinney, the actor who plays Jim Casy in the Steppenwolf production, sees parallels between the problem of the homeless in New York's East Village and the story of the Joads. A review by David Patrick Stearns connects Steinbeck's "surprisingly timely message" with how we "deal with holocaust." Like Kinney, Mimi Kramer, in her review in the *New Yorker,* claims that *The Grapes of Wrath* is about homelessness, but what she describes is a more general homelessness, which, in her opinion, characterizes all great American epics, including *Gone with the Wind, Moby-Dick,* and on another level *The Wizard of Oz.* Alan Brinkley's response to his own question of "Why Steinbeck's Okies Speak to Us Today" is that Steinbeck's message is of the importance of a "transcendent community" that Brinkley links to both modern radicalism and conservatism, citing former President George Bush's "thousand points of light" as a contemporary expression of a call to transcendent community.

Kinney, Stearns, Kramer, and Brinkley all posit acceptable explanations for the lasting quality of Steinbeck's novel. Each of their theories adds its own illumination to Steinbeck's story. And this is appropriate, because Steinbeck described *The Grapes of Wrath* as a five-layered book, explaining that "a reader will find as many as he can and won't find more than he has in himself."

I would like to suggest yet a different layer in Steinbeck's novel, a layer that, at Steinbeck's suggestion, I found in myself. It is a layer that, like the other layers, readers have found in themselves; it explains a significant portion of the book's continuing and universal appeal, because if *The Grapes of Wrath* is about homelessness, if it is about the exploitation of an underclass by the power structure, and if it is the American equivalent of the exodus from Egypt, as various writers have suggested, it is also the story of a quintessential American experience.

A UNIVERSAL EXPERIENCE

And it is more than that. For while the immigrant's experience can be categorized on a personal level and also be seen as a national paradigm, it is not just in America that *The Grapes of Wrath* endures. Steinbeck's pages communicate to a worldwide audience, as the Third International Steinbeck

Congress and the Steinbeck Conference held in October 1989 in Moscow illustrate. And while there are as many reasons for the novel's worldwide appeal as there are for its American appeal, perhaps the theme of the eternal immigrant is another reason why the story of the Joads speaks to such varying audiences. For the problems faced by immigrants are international. Peoples move, boundaries change, economic and political problems create migrations. The Oklahomans in California are like the Chinese in Malaysia, the Indians in South Africa, the Turkish in Germany, or the Algerians in France. Professor Jin Young Choi, speaking on "Steinbeck Studies in Korea" on the first day of the Third International Steinbeck Congress, commented on the parallels between Steinbeck's Okies and Korean farmers who moved to Manchuria. Her evocation of the empathy with which the Korean psyche, educated by the experiences of Korean immigrants in China, Japan, and Manchuria, is keyed to the suffering of the displaced provides yet another piece of evidence in the case I wish to build. My thesis, then, is that the Joads gain much of their literary cachet [a mark of quality] from the similarities of the problems suffered by immigrants everywhere. Their experience is universal. . . .

Steinbeck's awareness of this is communicated both subtly and pointedly. In chapter 19, one of the interchapters where he expresses the mood of the Californians during this period and their hostile attitude toward drought refugees, his narration leaves little doubt that the Oklahomans are perceived as aliens, not countrymen. Steinbeck depicts a scene where a deputy sheriff tramples the small, secret garden of one of the migrant workers. We enter the sheriff's thoughts as he kicks off the heads of turnip greens. "Outlanders," he thinks, "foreigners." His reason recoils from this untruth, but it is no match for his emotions, which rationalize his actions by explaining, "Sure, they talk the same language, but they ain't the same."

The sheriff is one individual, but in the narrative Steinbeck also imagines the thought patterns of the general community. In these passages is more evidence that the newcomers are considered foreigners. To excuse their brutality toward the migrants, the citizens who run the communities project a possible uprising among the Okies. In their collective paranoia, they fear that the farm laborers might retaliate against their harsh treatment, might march against their oppressors as "the Lombards did in Italy, as the Germans did in Gaul, and the Turks in Byzantium." Clearly, the images in the Californians' minds equate the Okies with foreigners.

Chapter 19 is one of the most clearly articulated instances in which Steinbeck's narrative demonstrates that he understood that the Oklahomans were more immigrant than migrant in the minds of his fellow Californians. But he also develops the idea dramatically through his narrative. In the Joad family scenes, he shows us the Joads experiencing what immigrants have borne throughout history. . . .

THE IMMIGRANT'S DREAM

At the heart of every immigrant's experience is a dream—a vision of hope that is embodied in his or her destination. Americans have long seen their country as the land of opportunity, and the vision carried in the hearts of most immigrants who have come here is of the *goldeneh medina*, a place where the streets are paved with gold. For every immigrant is impelled by the expectation of a better life at his or her journey's end. What else but such a vision could entice Haitians to brave stormy seas on rickety rafts, the Vietnamese boat people, the Marielitos [Cuban boat people], Mexican boys to allow themselves to be locked into suffocating boxcars? Similarly, the Joads embark upon a hazardous journey, their overburdened truck like a rickety raft, the Arizona and California deserts seas of sand rather than water. The gold at the end of their journey is embodied in the orange groves of California rather than the imagined gold-paved streets of New York. Ma's vision is of a place "never cold. An' fruit ever' place, an' people just bein' in the nicest places, little white houses in among the orange trees. . . . An' the little fellas go out an' pick oranges right off the tree." Ma's dream vision, where gold/oranges hang on the trees (lie in the streets) just for the taking, is an archetypal immigrant fantasy.

For Ma the oranges represent more than gold; they represent the luxury and nourishment of the Promised Land. In her vision, oranges are abundant "ever' place" and readily accessible, "right off the tree." Orange trees do not grow in Oklahoma, so oranges are also a bit of a delicacy. For my father, who was raised in Poland, the symbol was bananas, a great luxury in that cold country. When he was told that bananas were sold at five cents a stalk in Nicaragua, the country he first immigrated to, he thought it must be a land of unimagined luxury and abundance.

For Grampa Joad, in the novel, the synecdoche [a figure of speech that takes a part for the whole] is more biblical. California is where he can "get a whole bunch of grapes" and "squash 'em on my face an' let 'em run offen my chin." Fruit, be it oranges, grapes, or bananas, is a universal symbol for abundance and luxury. Maybe that is why the horn of plenty is filled with it.

STEREOTYPING AND PREJUDICE

The immigrant's dream is often unrealistic, and extravagant expectations can lead to bitter disappointment. Steinbeck foreshadows this in his novel. Even Ma, who acts as the cheerleader for the venture, has her moments of doubt. She says to Tom, "I'm scared of stuff so nice. I ain't got faith. I'm scared somepin ain' so nice about it." Faced with the reality of pulling up roots and leaving his and his ancestors' home ground, Grampa rejects his promised luxury: "I don't give a goddamn if they's oranges an' grapes crowdin' a fella outa bed even." The dream turns to ashes as the nourishing oranges and grapes become "winfall" peaches that, rather than providing sustenance, cause "the skitters." My father's bitter lesson came when, having bought several stalks of five-cent-bananas at the dock the minute his boat landed, he discovered that a stalk of bananas cost only two cents in the city. . . .

NAME CALLING

Another aspect of the immigrant experience that echoes from the pages of *The Grapes of Wrath* is the propensity for finding a derogatory term with which to label the new arrival. Contemporary sociology books define this as an "ethnophaulism." The term carries with it deprecatory stereotypes and negative images. And the world learned the term "Okies" from Steinbeck. The term became so well known that my immigrant father was bemused when I brought home what he referred to jokingly as an "Okie" to marry. He expected a rube, driving a laden-down jalopy. The image of the "Okie" as beaten-down loser was so pervasive that the Board of Regents of the University of Oklahoma came up with the idea of creating a championship football team as an antidote for the statewide depression caused by Steinbeck's book.

In the novel, Tom first hears the word from a man who, returning from California, tells him, "You never been called 'Okie' yet." Tom doesn't know what the word means. He asks, "Okie? What's that?" The man responds, "Well, Okie use' ta mean you was from Oklahoma. Now it means you're a dirty son-of-a-bitch. Okie means you're scum." Each immigrant group has experienced its share of such epithets, complete with the stereotypes that accompany them. The effect is soul-withering. Even the redoubtable Ma is unnerved by the epithet. Her interchange with the policeman who first uses the term on her illustrates both the negative effect of the name-calling and the fact that Ma sees herself as coming from a different country than his.

The policeman begins by saying to Ma, "We don't want none of you settlin' down here." Ma's response is anger. She picks up an iron skillet and advances on the man. When he loosens his gun, she rejoins, "Go ahead. . . . Scarin' women. I'm thankful the men folks ain't here. They'd tear you to pieces. *In my country* [emphasis mine] you watch your tongue." It is at this point that the man responds, "Well, *you ain't in your country* [emphasis mine] now. You're in California, an' we don't want you goddamn Okies settlin' down." Note that both Ma and the policeman see themselves as coming from different countries, not as citizens of the same country. At this point in the interchange Ma's advance is stopped. It is not the gun that stops her, but the effect of the name-calling: "She looked puzzled. 'Okies?' she said softly. 'Okies'." When the man leaves, Ma has to fight with her face to keep from breaking down. The effect is so devastating that Rose of Sharon pretends to be asleep.

Hungarians have been called "hunkies," Bohemians "bohunks," Chinese "chinks," and Italians "dagos." Ethnophaulisms exist for every kind of immigrant, regardless of race or country of origin. In scenes such as the one between Ma and the policeman, Steinbeck shows that he understands the effects of this kind of name-calling. He shows his Californians behaving toward the new arrivals in ways that are typical of the in-group's behavior toward the out-group. He is particularly adept at underlining the distance between the behavior of the out-group and the way that behavior is perceived by the in-group. This he does with caustic dramatic irony. In one instance, the reader has just finished a scene in which the Joads act unusually compassionately and charitably.

They, who have so few resources, give part of what they have to people who are neither kin nor longtime friends. Pa takes "two crushed bills" from his purse and leaves them, together with a half sack of potatoes and a quarter of a keg of salt pork that Ma has put by, for the Wilsons. After this remarkable act of charity, their next stop is a service station in Needles. The service station attendant does not see the Joads that Steinbeck has just shown the reader. He sees only their determination, which he translates into hardness, describing them to his helper as "a hard-looking outfit." His helper provides the stereotype: "Them Okies? They're all hard-lookin'." Then he goes on to make statements that reveal the depth of his prejudice, a prejudice expressed toward this group of Anglo-American migrants, but one remarkably similar to the prejudices expressed toward many immigrant groups.

One of the cruel ironies of the treatment of immigrant groups is that they are paid lower wages, given poorer working conditions, limited to uninhabitable living quarters, and then despised as being subhuman because they live as they do. Steinbeck has his service station boy say, "Them goddamn Okies got no sense and no feeling. They ain't human. A human being wouldn't live like they do. A human being couldn't stand it to be so dirty and miserable. They ain't a hell of a lot better than gorillas." The universality of this kind of negative stereotyping is almost too obvious for commentary. It is the kind of thinking that allows the killing of "gooks" because they aren't seen as human, the lynching of "niggers" because they are seen as an inferior species.

INHUMANE TREATMENT

Steinbeck shows numerous instances of the Okies being treated as less than human. Although Floyd, a man the Joads meet in the first Hooverville camp, does little more than ask the contractor about his license and pay scale, the deputy shoots at Floyd when he runs from possible incarceration. Only the most blatant disregard for the bystanders could produce such a response by the deputies, as lawmen are taught to hold their fire in a crowd. Steinbeck's narrative makes it clear that Floyd is dodging in and out of sight in a crowd of people when the deputy fires. The result is horrible. A woman's hand is shattered. This has no effect on the deputy, who "raised his gun again." At this point, Casy kicks him in the neck. The woman is hysterical, with blood oozing from her wound. When the rest of the deputy's group arrives and Casy tells them that the deputy hit a woman, they show no interest in her. Even when Casy says, "They's a woman down the row like to bleed to death from his bad shootin'" their response is: "We'll see about that later." After Casy reminds them a third time, they finally go to take a look. Their behavior, which up to this point is totally devoid of responsibility, is compounded by insensitivity and lack of humanity. They do not see a woman, another human being. They only see the "mess a .45 does make."

Because of their powerlessness and because they are seen as less than human, immigrants are often housed apart and in dehumanizing facilities. This has been true since medieval times, when immigrants were relegated to the outskirts of the city, the most dangerous area in those days because it was most vulnerable to attack. In an ironic reversal, today's most dangerous areas are the inner cities, where ghettos are most often located. This "segregation" or "ghettoization" is called "spatial segregation" in contemporary sociological studies. Steinbeck's Okies are subjected to this "spatial segregation." They are not allowed to settle where they like but are shunted to the Hoovervilles, impermanent shantytowns of tents and shacks. And even these miserable communities are seen as threatening by the xenophobic citizens. The first Hooverville the Joads stay in is burned so its inhabitants must move on. The burning of ghettos, or shtetls, was common, and was sometimes responsible for creating immigrants, as in the fictional Anatevka of *Fiddler on the Roof,* which had many real-life analogues.

When the migrant workers are given housing by the companies that hire them, the living conditions are appalling. Universally, living conditions and working conditions that immigrant and migrant workers must endure are disgraceful. The burning to death of the young garment workers who were locked up in the loft is a historical instance of the abusive working conditions immigrants suffered. When the Joads go to pick peaches, they are, for all intents and purposes, locked in. A police escort ushers them in, a guard with a shotgun sits at the end of each street, and when Tom tries to go outside the camp for a walk, a guard with a gun tells him he cannot leave the compound. The image is of a work camp—as in the Netherlands, where the Moluccans were housed in the concentration camps abandoned by the Nazis.

The house the Joads are assigned is one room for eight people, a room that smells of sweat and grease. Nor have the facilities for laboring immigrants changed much. If anything, they are worse. In a 1981 study, migrant housing is called "grotesque" and "nightmarish." The reporter says it is difficult to write about "without seeming to be melodramatic." Brent Ashabrenner, in a 1985 book about Haitians, Jamaicans, and Guatemalans who, with their families, are the contemporary Okies of Florida and the South, reports similar conditions.

THE PEOPLE GO ON

Steinbeck leaves his immigrant family devastated by death, desertion, and flood. The last scene—Rose of Sharon's selfless act of giving—used to fill me with impatience. How ridiculous to expect that this woman, whose lack of proper nutrition and care has produced a dead baby, should have enough nourishment to sustain a dying man. What a paltry symbolic act. And yet, history has proved Steinbeck's impulse unerring. For, as Ma prophesied, the people do go on. The Okies have survived. James Gregory, in . . . *American Exodus* [1989], charts the durability of the Okie subculture in California today.

Faced with seemingly insurmountable obstacles, immigrants the world over not only survive, but prevail. Michael Dukakis, the son of Greek immigrants, ran for president of the United States. Alberto Fujimori, son of Japanese immigrants to Peru, won the Peruvian presidency. Roberto Villareal, who as a boy picked cotton with his Mexican immigrant family in the fields of Texas, is now chairman of the Department of Political Science at the University of Texas at El Paso, my university. *The Grapes of Wrath* speaks to me, because *The Grapes of Wrath* speaks of me, an immigrant, who with my family experienced the pains and promise of immigration, an experience Steinbeck wrote of so tellingly in his story of the Joads.

The Weaknesses of a Great Novel

Harry T. Moore

Harry T. Moore's *The Novels of John Steinbeck: A First Critical Study* appeared in 1939, the year *The Grapes of Wrath* was published. In this excerpt, Moore, a distinguished literary critic, points out both the power and the limitations of the novel. Though he ultimately concludes that Steinbeck is a poet for the American underclass, Moore finds *The Grapes of Wrath* unconvincing in its use of everyday language, narrative, metaphors, and unnatural descriptions. He also criticizes what he perceives to be a lack of conflict in the novel and a weak ending that is never satisfactorily rounded off. Harry T. Moore is the author of books on D.H. Lawrence, Henry James, E.M. Forster, and Fyodor Dostoyevsky.

Since his first dip into local labor problems in *In Dubious Battle*, Steinbeck has become increasingly concerned with the social aspects of his California setting, which have provided the material for his latest novel, *The Grapes of Wrath* (April 1939). The articles Steinbeck wrote on the migratory laborers for the *San Francisco News* in 1936 lead directly to this new book; these articles were reprinted in a pamphlet two years later by the Simon J. Lubin Society of San Francisco, and a 1938 epilogue was added. This pamphlet, *Their Blood is Strong*, reveals how close—in sympathy and as an actual observer—Steinbeck is to his subject-matter. He has thoroughly explored the problems of the people he writes of, he understands these people, and his heart is with them. Besides the experience he had with them in California, he drove west from Oklahoma with some of them in 1937 and saw for himself the hardships that beset them on their western journey. . . .

Reprinted from Harry Thornton Moore, *The Novels of John Steinbeck: A First Critical Study* (Chicago: Normandie House, 1939), by permission of the author's Estate.

A MEMORABLE START

The Grapes of Wrath has a memorable beginning; the first chapter is at the top of Steinbeck's work. The dust storm comes in slowly, muffling the air and driving the people to their houses: "In the morning the dust hung like fog, and the sun was red as ripe new blood. All day the dust sifted down from the sky, and the next day it sifted down. An even blanket covered the earth. It settled on the corn, piled up on the tops of the fence posts, piled up on the wires; it settled on roofs, blanketed the weeds and trees. . . ." The whole chapter has a symphonic effect, one of the most impressive in Steinbeck: it gets the story under way with a slow, steady rhythm, a rhythm that pervades the book and matches the slow movement of the dispirited people. The pace stays too slow throughout the novel, so there is no real quickening into a crescendo, but in these early parts the slow rhythm seems to promise a story of grandeur and epic movement. . . .

REALISTIC LANGUAGE

Things people say in *The Grapes of Wrath* sometimes have a flavor of staginess because Steinbeck was trying to reproduce speech exactly. This presents a problem: complete literalness in such matters doesn't necessarily simulate life in literature. American speech has been successfully fused into creative prose by perhaps only one writer, Ernest Hemingway. Hemingway doesn't attempt literalness, but adapts the rudiments of American speech-rhythm to his personal sense of cadence. He is monotonous and repetitious, but deliberately so, and with telling effect. Although the speeches of his people have sufficient relation to their source so they could be fitted to American lips, they are nevertheless not automatic reproduction—they have their own identity. These speeches are Hemingway's own distinctive instrument and at the same time a living suggestion of American utterance. The most successful speech-reproductions in *The Grapes of Wrath* are when Steinbeck approximates this condition in the chapters where he is trying to convey a general effect rather than literal individual conversations. These chapters occur at frequent intervals throughout the book; they are devoted to generalized accounts of the moving body of people, of the factors that drove them forth, of the topography of their journey, of what they will find at the end of it. These sections are in some respects the best in the book; they never quite function so efficiently as they should because the contrapuntal chapters about the Joad family don't always have the continuous strength to carry them. If the central narrative were more forcefully concentrated, these choral chapters would be set off magnificently, given more meaning and volume. But although they don't realize their full accessory value, still they have a power in the way they catch the essential spirit of that sprawling westering movement. And they pick out its vocal overtones; there is at times a resemblance to [American poet] Carl Sandburg's *The People, Yes.* American names are named, places are mentioned, automobiles and native foods are identified. And all this is not literal speech reproduction, but a swelling musical suggestion of it that gives a far greater sense of "reality" than literal reporting. These chapters have an American resonance.

WEAKNESS OF THE JOAD NARRATIVE

Steinbeck had great material for the central narrative part of his story: perhaps he was too much aware of this, took too much for granted. For although these sections of the book are handled smoothly, well written for the most part, and crowded with living people, the main story never quite comes to life in the way it should. This may be partly because the Joad group is too well-balanced; even if Ma Joad and Tom are brought into focus oftener than the others, neither of them really arouses our fullest empathy. And there isn't a continuity of suspense, a mounting excitement, as there was in [Steinbeck's earlier novel] *In Dubious Battle.* Here the material is more maturely dealt with, the people and incidents are more plausible, there is greater scope, yet the story has no moving crisis. The book was not written with the passion that went into *In Dubious Battle,* and it lacks that novel's compulsion of participation.

WEAK PRESENTATION OF METAPHORS

Steinbeck's imagination was often fundamentally right when he was working out the problems of this book; he called up some excellent metaphors. But they are presented too deliberately, without spontaneity and passion, and they don't illuminate the text so intensely as they might. As an example, we may examine the passage about the tractors, the "snub-nosed monsters" invading Oklahoma, driving people off the land, cracking the houses and fences to splinters. There is this description of the driver and his work:

> The man sitting in the iron seat did not look like a man; gloved, goggled, rubber dust mask over nose and mouth, he was part of the monster, a robot in the seat. The thunder of the cylinders sounded through the country, became one with the air and the earth, so that earth and air muttered in sympathetic vibration. The driver could not control it—straight across country it went, cutting through a dozen farms and straight back. A twitch at the controls could swerve the cat', but the driver's hands could not twitch because the monster that built the tractor, the monster that sent the tractor out, had somehow got into the driver's hands, into his brain and muscle, had goggled him and muzzled him—goggled his mind, muzzled his speech, goggled his perception, muzzled his protest. He could not see the land as it was, he could not smell the land as it smelled; his feet did not stamp the clods or feel the warmth and power of the earth. He sat in an iron seat and stepped on iron pedals. He could not cheer or beat or curse or encourage the extension of his power, and because of this he could not cheer or whip or curse or encourage himself. He did not know or own or trust or beseech the land. If a seed dropped did not germinate, it was nothing. If the young thrusting plant withered in drought or drowned in a flood of rain, it was no more to the driver than to the tractor.

There is some good writing here, and originally the metaphor was cleverly conceived. But at last it comes to seem as if it were too coldly written down, the sentences are simply laid end to end, and the imaginative possibilities of the symbol don't come up living from the page. This should have been done in a few simple, warm strokes that would have made this goggled figure into a hideous and haunting demon. The effect would be double: there would be not only the horror of the despoliation of the land, there would also have been an unforgettably ghastly symbol of the doom that was hagriding the people of the story. . . .

NONAUTHENTIC WRITING

Sometimes in this book Steinbeck's writing-power fails, and he slips into the literary. The blood-ripe sun that was so vivid in an early passage about the dust storms appears to poor advantage in a later scene: "A large red drop of sun lingered on the horizon and then dripped over and was gone, and the sky was brilliant over the spot where it had gone, and a torn cloud, like a bloody rag, hung over the spot of its going." This kind of writing, which is essentially "indoor" and literary in contrast to the authentic natural descriptions Steinbeck is capable of, can spoil important parts of the story. It does so in the episode where Ma Joad goes down to Tom's hiding place to warn him that he is again in danger of being caught, this time for killing the vigilante who had murdered Casy. Ma, bringing him a plate of food, has to sneak out of the camp and go down to the place where Tom is hiding by the river. It is a moment of high suspense, but the suspense is impaired when we read: "Over the sky a plump black cloud moved, erasing the stars. The fat drops of rain scattered down, splashing loudly on the fallen leaves, and the cloud moved on and unveiled the stars again." This is strained, bookish writing, the stars being erased by a plump cloud, and so on, and there is a confused image with clouds being erased at one moment and unveiled the next. As yet the general health of Steinbeck's writing has not altogether overcome his inclination to the gaudy, and although these defects are being minimized, it is jarring to find them injuring passages that need sustained dramatic tension. . . .

A REVOLUTIONARY NOVEL

The Grapes of Wrath may become the *Uncle Tom's Cabin* of these migrant workers. It may do for them what [British novelist Charles] Dickens' *Nicholas Nickleby* did for the persecuted boys in small English board schools, what [American novelist Herman] Melville's *White Jacket* did for the sailors who were being flogged in the American fleet, what Upton Sinclair's *The Jungle* did towards cleaning up the meat-packing industry. *The Grapes of Wrath* will probably have a large sale, and in some quarters will certainly be a *succes de scandale*. As far as social implications go, it is perhaps the most persuasively revolutionary novel published in America, and it is in the van of the proletarian movement in literature, without officially being a part of that movement. In some sections of California the book will probably be sold under the counter, as *In Dubious Battle* was. *The Grapes of Wrath* consistently uses language that will give puritans the ecstasy of a good shock: but the Joads of life, so close to the most elemental manifestations of sex and death, know of no other way to speak. This novel has the displays of brutality usually found in a Steinbeck book; some of the natural deaths are gruesome enough (Ma Joad lying all night beside Granma's body, knowing Granma was dead but keeping it a secret so there would be no delay as the truck went over the oppressively hot desert)—and there are harsh killings. The book has an Old Testament grimness. . . .

AN EPIC NOVEL

The Grapes of Wrath has certain elements in common with classics other than the Bible—with the great sagas and with all tales of exile and wanderings and adventure. (It will be remembered how *Tortilla Flat* parodied some of these classics.) Because of their American clothing, the incidents in *The Grapes of Wrath* may seem to be no more than things that happened on an American journey, but regarded in outline most of them seem part of a vast *mythos*. One thing is certain: the author knows something of the form of the *Odyssey*, the *Divine Comedy*, *Don Quixote* [epic works by Homer, Dante, and Cervantes, respectively]. Attempts of this kind have been made in America before, though not so many as it would seem the bigness of the place should induce. . . . The only American who has successfully created life-in-literature on the scale of the great writers of the earth is Herman Melville: individuals fuse with the world of the [whaling ship] *Pequod* in that wild and mystic hunt after the white whale Moby-Dick. *The Grapes of Wrath* falls far short of such a book as that, not only because it lacks the intensity of a *Moby-Dick* but also because no compounding agent can bring the two elements of the story organically together. . . . There is a fundamental weakness in *The Grapes of Wrath*, and it is just this lack of force in the center of the story: it seems as if Steinbeck had done all in his power to give the novel verisimilitude and movement, had assembled all the required ingredients for a great book, and then failed to provide it with proportioned and intensified drama.

THE NOVEL LACKS CONFLICT

There is no vital conflict in *The Grapes of Wrath*. The story divides into two parts: first there is the departure from Oklahoma and the westward pilgrimage, then there is the California experience. This latter part remains static because it is a chronicle of the way the migratory workers are kicked around. No conflict is created because these trampled people don't fight back. It is a stirring picture of California's rotten social-economic-political conditions, and might be regarded as a deepening of the background material of *In*

Dubious Battle. But that presented a conflict in dramatic terms; the double implication at the end of *The Grapes of Wrath*—that life will go on, and that Tom will work for the common good—is too quiet to resolve the issues that have been raised.

AN UNSATISFACTORY ENDING

Several things in the story are never rounded off satisfactorily. The disappearance of Rosasharn's husband, Connie Rivers, leaves some unfinished business; it is too abrupt, and we feel we should not be through with Connie yet. The case of Noah Joad is somewhat similar, and his staying on at Needles, at the parched edge of California, has a false chime. Noah finds a river, and it lures him. His explanations are not convincing, and the writing is unreal: "Tom, I ain't a-gonna leave this here water. I'm a-gonna walk on down this here river. . . . No. It ain't no use. I was in that there water. An' I ain't a-gonna leave her. I'm a-gonna go now, Tom—down the river. I'll catch fish an' stuff, but I can't leave her. I can't . . . . You tell Ma, Tom." The story gets incredible here. Noah is not made of the same stuff as Lennie in [Steinbeck's novella] *Of Mice and Men*, but here he is talking as Lennie would have talked and doing what Lennie would have wanted to do. He walks away down the river through the willows, and Tom watches him; we never see Noah again. . . .

DOUBLE MEANINGS OF THE ENDING

It is Ma Joad's words that give the story the double implication of its ending. She has said "They ain't gonna wipe us out. Why, we're the people—we go on." And Rosasharn helps to prove this, for even if her own child has been born dead, Rosasharn can still give life. This final incident is not without the sense of contrivance which Steinbeck can't seem to get away from: the floods have to come to the Joads' box-car camp and drive them forth to the shelter of a dry barn where Rosasharn can be brought into contact with the starving man. But even though the incident is so obviously "planted," it is skillfully lifted into a symbol. It is out of [French writer Guy de] Maupassant, but while in his story the situation has a merely physical meaning, here the episode magnifies Ma Joad's statement of the life-principle: "We're the people—we go on."

The other phase of the ending is supplied by Ma Joad's

last visit to Tom. He will have to be a fugitive the rest of his life—if he ever gets into trouble and has his fingerprints taken, he will be sent back to Oklahoma to be imprisoned again for breaking parole. He has killed two men. He could easily become an outlaw like Pretty Boy Floyd, whom his mother speaks of: "I know'd Purty Boy Floyd's ma. He wasn't a bad boy. Jus' got drove in a corner." Tom is in a corner too, but instead of taking the easy way out, bitterness and frustration and banditry and murder, he has decided to work towards some of the things Casy was finding out before the defenders of liberty murdered him: Tom has been given a sense of social justice and he wants to work with people, organize them against the crushing system. He will fight the dubious battle to help lead his people out of the wilderness.

Whether Steinbeck will continue Tom's story or whether he will consider that all this is behind him and begin a new phase of his own career, only the future can tell. But this much is certain: up to this time he has gone farther than any other American writer towards being the poet of our dispossessed.

Flaws in *The Grapes of Wrath*

Frederick J. Hoffman

Frederick J. Hoffman's critical review of *The Grapes of Wrath* characterizes the novel's flaws. Hoffman finds the novel convincing on the literary level as an account of one family's migration to California, less successful as a symbolic work, and an utter failure as a philosophical statement. Steinbeck's attempt to make generalized observations about the nature of man in the interchapters imposes a false significance on the actions of his characters. Frederick Hoffman is a well-known critic who has written books on William Faulkner, F. Scott Fitzgerald, and Gertrude Stein.

The design of ... [*The Grapes of Wrath*], long and verbose as it is, may be reduced to three observable strategies: the realistic, the symbolic, the philosophical. On the first level, Steinbeck was capable of effective writing. His representation in individual scenes (when viewed in isolation) is very impressive. For the most part, he resists the temptation to overreach his opportunities. The seriousness of human crisis and the comedy of everyday issues are often quite economically given. In such passages as the following, he reveals a lesson well learned from [American novelist Ernest] Hemingway:

> Ahead of him, beside the road, a scrawny, dusty willow tree cast a speckled shade. Joad could see it ahead of him, its poor branches curving over the way, its load of leaves tattered and scraggly as a molting chicken. Joad was sweating now. His blue shirt darkened down his back and under his arms. He pulled at the visor of his cap and creased it in the middle, breaking its cardboard lining so completely that it could never look new again. And his steps took on new speed and intent toward the shade of the distant willow tree. At the willow he knew there would be shade, at least one hard bar of absolute shade thrown by the trunk, since the sun had passed its zenith.

At least here the details are self-contained; no one of them is incompatible with its very limited subject. And those sections of *The Grapes of Wrath* which remain free of large and false implication contain within themselves a remarkably well sustained narrative—held together as it is by the simple but convincing structural device of U.S. Highway 66. The next strategy is less successful, though even here it is sometimes quite well integrated with the first. The symbolic exertions of the author are, for the most part, violations of theme rather than successful extensions of it. The turtle carries too much of a burden; the tractor violates more than the land; Rose of Sharon's gesture at the novel's end is a curiously inept survival of the sex-land mysticism of [Steinbeck's earlier novel] *To a God Unknown*. In general the symbols are embarrassingly and awkwardly intrusive; more than that, they are quite unnecessary Whitmanian [after the American poet, Walt Whitman] raids upon the self-sufficient and concrete substance of the novel. Instead of emerging naturally and with due humility from the novel's material, they are added to it, or singled out from it for special, self-conscious attention.

FAILURE OF THE INTERCHAPTERS

The worst strategy of all, the philosophical, involves what are perhaps some of the most wretched violations of aesthetic taste observable in modern American fiction; they are the fictional version of [American poet Carl] Sandburg's strident *The People, Yes* (1936). For the most part they are contained within the fifteen short chapters of "philosophical" commentary, through which Steinbeck has tried to impose a false epic note upon what is basically a sound conception. Nor is he content merely to represent himself as a philosopher in these chapters; he occasionally also gives the Joads the privileges of the country sage. A study of the style, rhetoric, and intellectual content of the fifteen chapters reveals Steinbeck's writing at its worst and his mind at its most confused; trying, as he does so often, to stimulate the worst kind of intellectual pathos [sentimentality] and to force the reader into a recognition of false significance:

> For man, unlike any other thing organic or inorganic in the universe, grows beyond his work, walks up the stairs of his concepts, emerges ahead of his accomplishments. This you may say of man—when theories change and crash, when schools,

philosophies, when narrow dark alleys of thought, national, religious, economic, grow and disintegrate, man reaches, stumbles forward, painfully, mistakenly sometimes. Having stepped forward, he may slip back, but only half a step, never the full step back. This you may say and know it and know it.

STEINBECK'S REPLY TO THE CRITICS

In 1955 the Colorado Quarterly *invited Steinbeck to reply to two critical articles on* The Grapes of Wrath *that appeared in its pages. Despite asserting that he is not against literary criticism, Steinbeck's response mixes disdain and cynicism.*

Thank you for your very kind letter and your offer to make space available for my comment on the two recent articles on the *Grapes of Wrath* which have appeared in the *Quarterly.* I wish I could so comment but I have no opinions nor ideas on the subject. . . . I think it is a bunch of crap. As such I am not against it so long as it is understood that the process is a kind of ill tempered parlour game in which nobody gets kissed. What such an approach would do to a student beyond confusing him and perhaps making him shy away from reading, I have no idea. I do not read much criticism of my work any more. In the first place it is valueless as advice or castigation since the criticised piece is finished and I am not likely to repeat it. And in the second place, the intrafrontal disagreements only succeed in puzzling me. Recently a critic proved by parallel passages that I had taken my whole philosophy from a 17th century Frenchman of whom I had never heard. I usually know what I want to say and hope I have the technique to say it clearly and effectively. As Tennessee Williams once said, "I put it down that a way and that's the only way I know to put it down."

I don't think the *Grapes of Wrath* is obscure in what it tries to say. As to its classification and pickling, I have neither opinion nor interest. It's just a book, interesting I hope, instructive in the same way the writing instructed me. Its structure is very carefully worked out and it is no more intended to be inspected than is the skeletal structure of a pretty girl. Just read it, don't count it!

Please believe me when I say I have nothing against the scholarly or critical approach. It does seem to me to have very little to do with the writing or reading of books.

The writing of books is a lonely and difficult job, and it takes all the time I have.

John Steinbeck, "A Letter on Criticism," in *Steinbeck and His Critics: A Record of Twenty-Five Years,* eds. E.W. Tedlock Jr. and C.V. Wicker. Albuquerque: University of New Mexico Press, 1957.

Because this passage is so placed that we know Steinbeck intends it to be taken with the utmost seriousness, it is especially damaging in what it reveals of his intellectual poverty. That poverty of mind, which seems a common failure among a majority of naturalist writers, serves to weaken the effect of *The Grapes of Wrath* as a whole. This passage and its fellows, together with the inappropriate mutterings of Ma and Tom Joad and of Casy, force the reader away from what are the essentially good sections of the novel: those parts of it in which Steinbeck has exercised (almost unwittingly, it seems) the caution and factual decorum demanded by the material. Aside from the very quiet, subdued heroics of ordinary man in critical situations, there are the heroics forced upon him by an author unsure of his subject and confused over what he should make of it.

Steinbeck's Pulitzer Prize

John Hohenberg

In 1940 *The Grapes of Wrath* was awarded the
Pulitzer Prize for fiction. In this excerpt from his
book *The Pulitzer Prizes,* John Hohenberg relates
that the selection was not an easy one, with two
prominent members of the Pulitzer advisory board
coming out strongly against the novel. Nevertheless,
other members prevailed and Steinbeck won the
award at the height of his career. The Pulitzer served
as a confirmation that Steinbeck had indeed become
a major American novelist. John Hohenberg has
worked as a journalist and taught at Columbia University. His other books include *The Professional
Journalist, Foreign Correspondence: The Great Re-
porters and Their Times* and *The News Media: A Journalist Looks at His Profession.*

John Steinbeck is scarcely considered today [in 1974] to be a
revolutionary force in American literature. But in the 1930s,
when labor organizers were appealing to the discontented in
a suffering land and some of the more frightened captains of
industry saw anarchy in every New Deal reform of consequence, the affluent conservatives viewed Steinbeck's proletarian novels with a certain degree of suspicion. Although
his style was graceful and engaging and although he was not
afraid to apply the leavening touch of humor to his grimmest
situations, he did not have a very good press on the whole.
The liberal critics liked him, it is true, but their largely conservative editors had distinct reservations. His progress,
therefore, was not as swift and his talent was not as quickly
recognized as it should have been. . . .

Steinbeck's first three books, his introduction to American
literature, were modestly received and attracted little public

Reprinted from *The Pulitzer Prizes,* by John Hohenberg, by permission of the publisher. Copyright © 1959, Columbia University Press.

attention. But with *Tortilla Flat* in 1935, *In Dubious Battle* in 1936, and *Of Mice and Men* in 1937, he established himself as a writer of consequence. After the publication of *The Grapes of Wrath*, in 1939, he was recognized as an American writer of the first rank, for this powerful tale of the migration of the Dust Bowl Okies to California went to the heart of the nation. If it tore holes in the American dream, it did nothing more than tell the truth about what had happened to millions of Americans during the Depression. If it was tough and coarse and profane, that was because its people were tough and coarse and profane. Although, by the standards of the 1970s, its profanity and vulgarity were mild, indeed.

To the [Pulitzer Prize] jury of Professors Krutch, Fletcher, and Lovett, *The Grapes of Wrath* was the book of the year and there was no argument about it. In his report, Krutch wrote: "We are unanimously agreed to recommend as our first choice *The Grapes of Wrath* by John Steinbeck. Despite the fact that it is marred by certain artistic blemishes, this novel has, we believe, excellences which make it the most powerful and significant of all the works submitted for our consideration."

When the report was distributed to the Advisory Board, two of the members were outraged. One of them, predictably enough, was Walter M. Harrison of the Oklahoma City *Daily Oklahoman* and the other was Robert Lincoln O'Brien of the Boston *Herald*. Both wrote letters to try to influence their colleagues against *The Grapes of Wrath* in advance of the Advisory Board meeting of May 3, 1940.

Harrison appeared to consider the book a slur on the people of his state, for he wrote:

> Nothing we can do will add or detract from the success of the publication. But the seal of the Pulitzer selection will write an approbation of smut in contemporary work that I am not quite willing to participate in. Such a decision would encourage more efforts in erotica by a host of authors writing for the market and promote a false sense of value with the immature reader which surely is neither enlightening nor constructive.

> While a segment of the migrants probably are of the moral and mental level of some of the Joads and their unfortunate neighbors, there is another unit, clean in their habits and minds, decent in their living and speaking. I do not know which is the larger class. This is a factual fault which should be considered. The errors of locale, the quarrel about the cause of the problem, the lack of a solution, are too trivial to carry weight.

I do not wish to confine juvenile reading to the Elsie Dinsmore [the main character in a series of Christian stories by Martha Finley] books, neither am I willing to help elevate cocktail hour wit and the filth of the jungle to the dignity of immortal literature.

O'Brien took it from there, questioning whether employers in California were as hard-hearted as *The Grapes of Wrath* made them out to be:

> I note the recommendation in reference to *The Grapes of Wrath.* I wonder if the jury has given any consideration to the question whether the main thesis of that book, which is that employers have allured the multitude into California into such numbers as to keep the wages depressed—is true? I read some articles in the New York *Times* several weeks ago in which the investigator reported quite emphatically that the charge is not true, that the LaFollette Civil Liberties Committee could not find anything of the sort, although it would have liked obviously to do so. I note that Mr. [William Randolph] Hearst refers to the book in his column as *Grapes of Rot.*

> I wonder if we have no responsibility for the fundamental verities involved in a matter of this kind? I wonder if it is not the business of the juries to tell us how this work does square with the fundamental verities? If somebody wrote a corresponding book based upon the thesis of the innocence of [political anarchists and convicted murderers] Sacco and Vanzetti I would have opposed the award because I do not think they were innocent. Why is not the same issue involved here?

When the Board met, there was a new chairman, Joseph Pulitzer, for his brother, Ralph, who had held the post so often from the outset, had died in the intervening year. The two objectors were in attendance, as was President Butler and all save one member who had been excused, Stuart H. Perry of the Adrian (Mich.) *Telegram.* There is no record of the discussion of the fiction award, but it must have been lively. In the end, however, Messrs. Harrison and O'Brien were unable to stop Steinbeck any more than [American author] Hamlin Garland had been able in the earliest years of the prize to stop [American playwright] Eugene O'Neill. When the award was voted by the university Trustees and made public, it was received with universal approval. For, as Malcolm Cowley wrote in the *New Republic, The Grapes of Wrath,* stands "very high in the category of great angry books like *Uncle Tom's Cabin* that have aroused a people to fight against intolerable wrongs."

The Pulitzer Prize served to confirm John Steinbeck's

stature as a major American novelist. However, since he was 38 years old when he received the award and at the high point of his productive and distinguished career, it is doubtful that the award had any particular impact on his fortunes. In fact, even though he received the Nobel Prize for Literature in 1962, his best work had been done long before and *The Grapes of Wrath* marked his peak. It is not often that a prize dovetails so neatly with the finest work of an artist's career, but this was what made the 1940 fiction award to *The Grapes of Wrath* all the more notable.

The Grapes of Wrath Fifty Years Later

Studs Terkel

In his introduction to the fiftieth-anniversary edition of *The Grapes of Wrath*, Studs Terkel, perhaps America's best-known oral historian, applies to Steinbeck's novel the method that made him famous. On a road trip in 1987, Terkel interviewed Americans on the significance of *The Grapes of Wrath*. His essay mixes their commentary with quotations from the novel, as he arrives at the conclusion that, even a half century later, the novel is as relevant as ever. Terkel's politics are on display as he, like Steinbeck, celebrates government's ability to solve problems and implies that much of the criticism of the novel centers on political and financial issues more than on the writing itself. Studs Terkel is the author of the Pulitzer Prize-winning *The Good War* (1985), *Working* (1974), *Hard Times: An Oral History of the Great Depression* (1970), and numerous other works.

It is 1988. We could see the face on the Six O'clock News. It could be a Walker Evans or Dorothea Lange shot [depression-era photographers], but that's fifty years off. It is a face of despair, of an Iowa farmer, fourth generation, facing foreclosure. I've seen this face before. It is the face of Pa Joad, Muley Graves, and all their lost neighbors, tractored out by the cats.

In the eyes of Carroll Nearmyer, the farmer, is more than despair; there is a hardly concealed wrath: as there was in the eyes of his Okie antecedents.

> Sure, cried the tenant farmers, but it's our land. We were born on it, and got killed on it, and we died on it. Even if it's no good, it's still ours. That's what makes it ours—being born on it, working on it, dying on it. That makes ownership, not a paper with numbers on it.
>
> (*The Grapes of Wrath*, chapter 5)

Listen to Carroll Nearmyer. I had visited his farm, twenty-four miles southeast of Des Moines. It was a soft, easy twilight in May 1987: "There was several times I had the gun to my head and she didn't know it. And then I got damn mad. I got to thinkin' about it and I got madder. These people don't have the right to do this to me! I have worked, I have sweated, and I have bled. I have tried out there to keep this place goin'. And then they tried to take it away from me!"

DRIVING INTO THE NOVEL

During a trip in 1987 through Iowa and Minnesota, I saw too many small towns with too many deserted streets that evoked too many images of too many rural hamlets of the Great Depression. I could not escape the furrowed faces and stooped frames of John Steinbeck's people. It was a classic case of life recapitulating art. The work of art, in this instance, caught more than people; it was their "super-essence" (Steinbeck's word).

It was a flash forward fifty years. The boarded-up stores and houses. The abandoned jalopies. The stray dog. The pervasive silence. "It's both a silence of protest and a silence of acceptance," observed my companion, who was doing the driving.

> The men were silent and they did not move often. And the women came out of their houses to stand beside their men— to feel whether this time the men would break. The women studied the men's faces secretly, because the corn could go, as long as something else remained.
>
> (*The Grapes of Wrath*, chapter 1)

What was that something else? It had something to do with respect for Self; sought from those dear to him and at least a semblance of it demanded from the Others. It was something he had to husband and preserve by himself, alone. Therein lay the fatal flaw; a fault he had to discover the hard way.

A half century later, Carolyn Nearmyer, Carroll's wife, recognized it. "The women are apt to talk to other farm wives about their problems, rather than sit down with their husbands. If I was to come up with a suggestion, he'd get very upset. It was not that I did not know as much as he did. It was just he was keeping it inside himself."

Ma Joad knew it, too. Though in her good-bye to Tom, she says, "I don' un'erstan', I don' really know," she does know.

Her generous heart gives the lie to her words. In Tom's reply, Preacher Casy's transcendental vision comes shining through:

> Maybe like Casy says, a fella ain't got a soul of his own, but only a piece of a big one—and then. . . . Then I'll be all around in the dark. I'll be ever'where—wherever you look. Wherever they's a fight so hungry people can eat, I'll be there. Wherever they's a cop beatin' up on a guy, I'll be there. Why, I'll be in the way guys yell when they're mad an'—I'll be in the way kids laugh when they're hungry an' they know supper's ready. An' when our folks eat the stuff they raise an' live in the houses they build—why, I'll be there.
>
> (*The Grapes of Wrath*, chapter 28)

A MUSICAL ARCHITECTURE

There are constant variations on this theme throughout *The Grapes of Wrath,* as in a symphony. The novel is constructed more like a piece of music rather than mere prose. It is not unlike [American architect] Frank Lloyd Wright's approach to architecture. As Bach and Beethoven were ever with the architect as he conceived buildings, as he reflected on the vision of his *lieber meister* [master], Louis Sullivan [Wright's mentor], so as we learn from the journal he kept during the book's composition, John Steinbeck was listening to the lushness of [composers] Tchaikovsky and the dissonance of Stravinsky, while he traveled with the Joads and their fellow tribesmen.

And when there was a pause in the recorded music, there was still a sort of rhythm: the incessant bup-bup-bup of the washing machine. Always, there was the beat, as though it were the beat of a throbbing heart, caught and held by these uprooted people whom he had come to know so well. "I grew to love and admire the people who are so much stronger and braver and purer than I am," [Steinbeck wrote].

In the musical architecture of the book are point and counterpoint. Each chapter, recounting the adventures of the individual family, the Joads, is followed by a brief contrapuntal [more than one melody at a time] sequence: the tribe, the thousands of Okie families on the move. The one, the many, all heading in the same direction. The singular flows into the plural, the "I" into the "We." It is an organic whole.

Organic was Wright's favorite word. The work had to flow naturally, whether it were a building or a book. Everything was of one piece, as the fingers on a hand, the limbs on a tree. It was not accidental that Wright's Imperial Hotel withstood the Tokyo earthquake of 1924. It was not accidental that *The Grapes of Wrath* has withstood another earthquake.

Preacher Casy's vision, as revealed to Tom Joad, was presaged by earlier variations on the theme. During the journey to California, twenty or so Okie families rested at a campsite, near a spring:

> In the evening a strange thing happened; the twenty families became one family, the children were the children of all. The loss of a home became one loss, and the golden time in the West was one dream. And it might be that a sick child threw despair into the hearts of twenty families, of a hundred people; that a birth there in a tent kept a hundred people quiet and awestruck through the night and filled a hundred people with the birth-joy in the morning.
>
> (*The Grapes of Wrath,* chapter 17)

And, finally, at saga's end, comes the breath-stopping incident in the barn. Outside, are the torrential rains and floods. Inside, Rose of Sharon, having lost her baby, offers her mother's milk to the starving stranger. It is much like an olden Childe ballad[1]—the stunning last verse. And yet so natural.

There were doubts expressed by friends who had read the manuscript. Why a stranger? Steinbeck knew why intuitively. The impulse was right, organically so. It fit like—well, the fingers on a hand, the limbs on a tree.

This book is more than a novel about an epic journey in an overcrowded, heavy-laden old Dodge jalopy across Highway 66, across hot desert sands, on toward Canaanland, the land of milk and honey; and further on toward disillusion and revelation. It is an anthem in praise of human community. And thus survival. . . .

DUST BOWL CONDITIONS IN 1988

During my Minnesota farmland trip in 1987, my companion points toward a barren field that appears endless. There are vast spaces that offer the odd appearance of crowds of baldheads. The color—the pallor—is a sickly, sandy gray.

"All those acres," she says, "not a tree, not a blade of grass. Nothin' to stop the wind from blowin' across. When you lose the farm, they bulldoze the grove down. Our land is very vulnerable. It's now dry and wide open to Mother Nature to do with as she pleases. There's six inches of topsoil left. It used to be six feet. Multiply this—these white tops—by hundreds

---

1. a narrative poem about a young man training to be a knight

of thousands of acres, all of a sudden, with a dry spell and drought and a wind, you've got a dust storm. Will it happen again? People are beginning to talk about it." Simultaneously, we mumble: "*The Grapes of Wrath.*" The drought of 1988 has underscored our mutual apprehension of the year before and the aching relevance of Steinbeck's book.

When asked, "What is the best novel you read in 1988?", the reply comes easy: *The Grapes of Wrath.* The third time around merely adds to its dimension. Dorothy Parker, at the time of its publication in 1939, called it "the greatest American novel I have ever read." She'll get no argument in these quarters.

THE THIRTIES AND THE EIGHTIES

The eighties, we have been informed, [were] distinguished by a mean-spiritness that has trickled down from high places, by an ethic of every man for himself, by a disdain for those up against it. It reveals itself even in our idiomatic language: Victims are defined as "losers." The word, with its new meaning, has become as common—and as popular—as "bottom line." Since there is obviously no room for "losers" at the top, there is no bottom for them either. The Joads would indubitably have fallen into that dark recess; as millions of our dispossessed fall today.

An Appalachian woman of my acquaintance puts it more succinctly: "People are made to feel ashamed now if they don't have anything. Back then, I'm not sure how the rich felt. I think the rich were as contemptuous of the poor then as they are now. But among the people that I knew during the Depression, we all had an understanding that it wasn't our fault. It was something that had happened to the machinery."

It isn't that the thirties lacked for meanness of spirit. God knows, the Joads and their uprooted fellows encountered it all the way. And then some. Aside from the clubs of the vigilantes, the maledictions of the big growers, and the stony cold of the banks, there were people like Joe Davis's boy.

As the caterpillar tractors rolled on and smashed down the homely shacks of the tenant farmers, they were driven by the sons of neighbors.

> The man sitting in the iron seat did not look like a man; gloved, goggled, rubber dust mask over nose and mouth, he was part of the monster, a robot in the seat. . . .
>   After a while, the tenant who could not leave the place came out and squatted in the shade beside the tractor.

"Why, you're Joe Davis's boy!"

"Sure."

"Well, what you doing this kind of work for—against your own people?"

"Three dollars a day. . . . I got a wife and kids. We got to eat. Three dollars a day, and it comes every day."

"That's right", the tenant said. "But for your three dollars a day, fifteen or twenty families can't eat at all. Nearly a hundred people have to go out and wander on the roads for your three dollars a day. Is that right?"

And the driver said, "Can't think of that. Got to think of my own kids. . . . Times are changing, mister, don't you know?"

(*The Grapes of Wrath*, chapter 5)

Fifty years later, the wife of the Iowa farmer tells this story. It had happened to her a month or so before our encounter: "When the deputy came out to take our stuff away from us, I asked him, 'How can you go home and face your family?' I happen to know he has an eight-year-old girl too. 'How can you sleep tonight knowing that someday this could be you?' He said, 'If I didn't do it, somebody else would be here. To me, it's just a job.' To me, that's heartless people. I wouldn't do that to somebody just because I needed the money."

Joe Davis's boy has always been around. From his point of view, it's quite understandable. It's every man for himself, buddy. In the eighties, there is considerably less onus attached to his job. Who wants to be a "loser"?

Yet, the Joads, for all their trials, found something else en route to California; and even before the trek began. We first meet Tom, just paroled from MacAlester pen.

The hitch-hiker stood up and looked across through the windows. "Could ya give me a lift, mister?"

The driver looked quickly back at the restaurant for a second. "Didn' you see the *No Riders* sticker on the win'shield?"

"Sure—I seen it. But sometimes a guy'll be a good guy even if some rich bastard makes him carry a sticker."

The driver, getting slowly into the truck, considered the parts of this answer. If he refused now, not only was he not a good guy, but he was forced to carry a sticker, was not allowed to have company. If he took in the hitch-hiker, he automatically a good guy and also he was not one whom any rich bastard could kick around. He knew he was trapped, but he couldn't see a way out. And he wanted to be a good guy.

(*The Grapes of Wrath*, chapter 2)

I ran into Sam Talbert, a trucker out of West Virginia, a few months before writing this introduction. "It scares me sometimes thinkin' people are never goin' to learn. I sometimes get to thinkin' people's gettin' too hard-hearted. There's no trust in anybody. Used to be, hitchhiking, you'd get a ride. Now they're afraid they'll be robbed, but people has always been robbed all their life. So it's hard for me to pass up a hitchhiker."

A Forgotten Past

Sam may be on to something. It's not so much not learning as it is tribal memory that's lost. A past, a history has been erased as effortlessly as chalk on a blackboard is erased. It's easy to decry the young clod who says, "A Depression to me is when I can't sit down on my chaise lounge and have a beer and this boob tube in my face." Too easy, perhaps.

The young Atlanta woman bites closer to the core of the apple. "Depression tales were almost like fairy tales to me. The things they teach you about the Depression in school are quite different from how it was. You were told people worked hard and somehow things got better. You never hear about the rough times. I feel angry, as though I were protected from my own history."

When World War Two ended the Great Depression and postwar prosperity, as well as God, blessed America, millions who had all their lives lived on the razor's edge suddenly experienced a security they had never before enjoyed. It was much easier then to suffer amnesia than to remember the dark times of the thirties.

It was so even for the sons and daughters of Okies.

The exquisite irony has not been lost on Jessie De La Cruz. Her family of farm workers has been at it since the thirties. Her hunger has always been Okie hunger. "We worked the land all our lives, so if we ever owned a piece of land, we felt we could make it." Perhaps that's why Muley Graves stubbornly, mulishly stayed on even though nothing remained but dusty old dust.

Perhaps that's why Jessie was so stunned by the forgettery of those who may have shared her experience, or whose mothers and fathers certainly did. "There's a radio announcer here in Fresno. He always points out, 'I was an Okie. I came out here and I made it. Why can't these Chicanos make it?'" The man at the mike could be little Winfield, the ten-year-old kid of Ma and Pa Joad, Tom's baby brother.

An elderly seamstress, who has seen hard times all her life, thinks this may be more than wild conjecture. "People fergits. I've know'd people lost someone in the war, they gits a little money an' they fergits. I've know'd Depression people, they fergits so easy.". . .

THE HARD TRUTH

The hard truth captured in *The Grapes of Wrath* was corroborated several months later with the publication of *Factories in the Field: The Story of Migratory Labor in California*. It was the work of Carey McWilliams, the state's Commissioner of Immigration and Housing: a rare public servant.

Steinbeck *had* to have it just right; there was to be not even the slightest error. He knew that the powerful growers, represented by the Associated Farmers, would be infuriated by the book. They were. "The Associated Farmers have begun an hysterical personal attack on me both in the papers and a whispering campaign. I'm a Jew, a pervert, a drunk, a dope fiend."

In his journal, he tells of a friendly sheriff warning him against staying in hotel rooms alone. "The boys got a rape case set for you. A dame will come in, tear off her clothes, scratch her face and scream and you try to talk yourself out of that one. They won't touch your book but there's easier ways."

They did touch his book. They did more than that. On a couple of occasions, they burned it in his home town. Today, Salinas [Steinbeck's birthplace in California] named a library after him and the Chamber of Commerce takes pride in being "Steinbeck Country."

The battle is not quite over. Today, *The Grapes of Wrath*, the master work of a Nobel Laureate, is the second most banned book in our school and public libraries.

It isn't the language. The colloquial profanities are mild indeed, certainly by today's standards. It must be something else. What? Perhaps the author has offered the reason: "I am completely partisan on the idea of working people to the end that they may eat what they raise, wear what they weave, use what they produce, and share in the work of their hands and heads." Tom Joad's vision was John Steinbeck's vision; a subversive impulse in some quarters.

DEMOCRACY AT WORK

If you were to choose the one episode that most disturbed the powerful, it may be the one that appears in the government camp sequence. After the Joads had left the wretched Hooverville, about to be burned down by the vigilantes, they came upon this place. As Tom checks in for the family, he is informed:

> "Folks here elect their own cops. . . . There's five sanitary units. Each one elects a Central Committeeman. Now that committee makes the laws. What they say goes."
>
> "S'pose they get tough", Tom said.
>
> "Well, you can vote 'em out jus' as quick as you vote 'em in." ". . . Then there's the ladies. They keep care of the kids an' look after the sanitary units. If your ma isn't working, she'll look after the kids for the ones that are working, an' when she gets a job—why, there'll be others. . . ."
>
> "Well, for christ's sake! Why ain't there more places like this?"
>
> "You'll have to find that out for yourself."
>
> (*The Grapes of Wrath*, chapter 21)

That Steinbeck captured the "feeling tone," as well as the literal truth, of a resettlement camp has since been underscored by the testimony of John Beecher, the southern poet. He himself managed such a camp for black sharecroppers in the Florida Everglades:

"When the day came to open, we just opened the gate and let anybody in that wanted to come in. No references or anything like that. It was enough for us that a family wanted to live there. We didn't hire guards either and nobody carried a club or a pistol in all that camp that held a thousand people.

"We just got them altogether and told them it was their camp. And there wouldn't be any laws, except the ones they made for themselves through their elected Council. The Council said a man couldn't beat his wife up in camp. And when a man came in drunk, he was out by morning. They had to pay their rent and out of it came money for the nursery school. And they started a co-op, without a dollar in it that the people didn't put up.

"Some of the men and women on that Council couldn't so much as write their names. Remember these were just country people off sharecrop farms in Georgia and Alabama. Just ordinary cotton pickers, the kind planters say would ruin the country if they had the vote. All I know is: My eyes have seen democracy work."

Let that serve as a brief resumé of Chapter Twenty-one of *The Grapes of Wrath*.

No wonder the Associated Farmers and their friends in Congress were so furious. (For the record: Of all the New Deal agencies, the Resettlement Administration, responsible for these camps, was the most bitterly attacked in Congress and in the press.) No wonder Peggy Terry felt otherwise.

PROUD OF THE POOR

Peggy had come out of western Kentucky. She had barely finished fifth grade. The Great Depression was her teacher. She had hard-traveled the highways and dirt roads, worked in the fields, slept in barns, her skinny young husband by her side, and, like Rose of Sharon, was big with child.

She remembers the day somebody handed her a well-thumbed paperback. ". . . And when I read *Grapes of Wrath,* that was like reliving my whole life. I was never so proud of poor people before as I was after I read this book."

I imagine John Steinbeck would have valued that critique as much as the Nobel Prize for Literature he won in 1962.

Censorship and *The Grapes of Wrath*

Lee Burress

According to Lee Burress, Steinbeck is one of the most censored novelists of the twentieth century. Attempts to censor *The Grapes of Wrath* began almost from the date of its publication and have continued to the present. Many of these attempts stem from misguided notions that the novel advocates communism or atheism. Burress dismisses these charges, which he suggests stem from a misreading of the book. Lee Burress has taught at the University of Wisconsin–Stevens Point. He is the author of several studies on censorship, including *The Battle of the Books: Literary Censorship in the Public Schools, 1950–85*.

In February 1980 the school board of Kanawha, Iowa, a small city in the northwestern part of Iowa, voted unanimously to ban *The Grapes of Wrath* from use in a sophomore English class. The book was allowed to remain in the school library. The action was taken as a result of a complaint by a parent who was vice-president of the local bank. The bank officer complained that the book was "profane, vulgar, and obscene," according to a report in the Des Moines *Register*.

It is an interesting coincidence that approximately at the same time the book was removed from use in the English class at Kanawha, the Sioux City Diocese of the Roman Catholic Church issued a report concerning land ownership patterns in Iowa after two years of study. The report stated that in the 14 northwestern counties of Iowa, 77% of the land was owned by absentee owners. It is probably coincidental that a banker should attack *The Grapes of Wrath* for being "profane, vulgar, and obscene" and ignore the Jeffersonian agrarianism that runs through the book. Steinbeck's charge

Reprinted from Lee Burress, "*The Grapes of Wrath:* Preserving Its Place in the Curriculum," in *Censored Books: Critical Viewpoints,* edited by Nicholas Karolides, Lee Burress, and John M. Kean, by permission of The Scarecrow Press. Copyright © 1993 by Nicholas Karolides, Lee Burress, and John M. Kean.

that capital is used to buy big tractors and drive farmers off the land may not have been apparent to the banker who complained about the book. But it is ironic that a novel which has such a theme as one of its organizing principles should be forbidden in a part of the country where traditionally the family farm has seemed to be a dominant feature of life.

A FREQUENTLY CENSORED BOOK

However, the effort to censor this book, based on a failure to understand it, or perhaps to understand it too well, began as soon as the book was published in 1939. Attacks on the book were not confined to California, or to Oklahoma, but occurred across the entire United States. Successful efforts were made to censor the book in public libraries in Kansas City, Buffalo, and in many other places. Several copies were burned in St. Louis. The attacks have continued, making Steinbeck one of the two or three most frequently censured and censored novelists of the twentieth century. The attacks were no doubt stimulated by the immediate popularity of the book in 1939, a popularity which has continued across the decades. By 1979 the book had had more than 40 printings in the United States and over 20 printings in England.

The Grapes of Wrath illustrates [British poet John] Milton's principle in the *Areopagitica* that "books are not absolutely dead things but contain a potency of life in them to be as active as that soul was whose progeny they are. . . ." The potency of *The Grapes of Wrath* grows out of the substantial degree of success that Steinbeck arrived at in creating a significant work of fiction from a major episode of American history, the depression and drought years of the 1930s. . . .

PRESERVING THE FAMILY FARM

[Critic] Frederick Ives Carpenter suggested, not long after the book's publication, that a number of the most characteristic American ideas appeared in the book—"the mystical transcendentalism of [American writer and philosopher] Emerson," "the earthy democracy of Walt Whitman," the "pragmatic instrumentalism of William James and John Dewey." Other readers have seen in the book the agrarian philosophy of Thomas Jefferson—a faith in the small farm that has strongly influenced our society. It was agrarianism

CONTINUED OBJECTIONS TO THE NOVEL

The blunt language of The Grapes of Wrath *causes the novel to be censored in school districts.*

In the spring of 1990, elementary school officials in San Diego, California, ordered a children's mural to be painted over because it showed banned books, including *The Grapes of Wrath*, used as a stairway to the wonders of the universe. A few teachers and parents claimed that such books were not appropriate for elementary school students to see. The artist who had supervised the children who painted the mural said:

> I knew the vice principal was upset because she called me to tell me that the book titles were not appropriate, but I never knew they had painted them over because I never gave them permission to do that. My feeling was that, if the kids can read that well, they ought to be able to read the books if they want.

In 1991, a parent in the Greenville County, South Carolina, School District objected to *The Grapes of Wrath* and two other books on the high school reading lists. The complaint said the books contained profanity and sexual innuendo and used God's name in vain. Despite the long-standing policy of offering alternative reading to objectors, the removal of the books was demanded. The school board of trustees accepted a review committee's decision to retain the three novels. One of the school trustees who had voted to remove the books explained, "I know you all are looking at this from an educational viewpoint but I have to look at it from whether it's right or wrong." A county legislator called another trustee and threatened to oppose tax revenues for the school district if she did not vote to remove the books. The controversy spread when the objector circulated lists of other allegedly profane books in the community and succeeded in getting over 2,000 signatures on a petition to ban the books. Nonetheless, the majority of parents, students, and teachers supported the continued use of the books.

In 1992, a parent in Midland, Michigan, objected to the use of *The Grapes of Wrath* in an eleventh-grade English class because of "references to sexual adventures," "581 curse words," and "283 cases of taking the Lord's name in vain." The school provided an alternative reading assignment to the student, but the parent said no student should be allowed to read it. Because the objector declined to file a formal written complaint, the school board did not act on her request to ban the book.

Herbert N. Foerstel, *"The Grapes of Wrath* by John Steinbeck" in *Banned in the U.S.A.: A Reference Guide to Book Censorship in Schools and Public Libraries.* Westport, CT: Greenwood Press, 1994.

that led to the homestead laws passed by the Republican Party when Abraham Lincoln was president, and that lay back of a variety of twentieth century efforts to assist farmers and protect the family farm.

No feature of the book is better illustrative of the tendency of the American novel to protest the conflict between American ideals and American practice than the novel's agrarianism. The Joads have as a major motivation their desire to own a piece of land, where they can raise the grapes of plenty, enough so that Pa Joad can squash the grapes across his face and feel the juice run down his chin, a destiny he is not to achieve.

The essential reality of the Joads' predicament is demonstrated by the fact that between 1940 and 1980 the number of American farms declined from 6 million to $2^1/_4$ million. Millions of Americans in that period left their farms for life elsewhere, as the Joads left their Oklahoma home. That migration of millions of people from rural areas to the city affected the United States in many ways—increasing crime and welfare on the one hand, and providing a ready force of factory workers on the other. Few people note that, as the novel implies, we pay for our food not only at the grocery store, but also in taxes caused by crime and welfare.

It is an ironic possibility that if all the political and editorial language calling for the preservation of the family farm were printed in a single set of volumes, it might exceed the attacks on *The Grapes of Wrath*. But it is doubtful that any other American novelist has so vigorously upheld the ideal of the American family farm or so artistically protested the failure of our society to make that ideal possible in reality.

MISREADING THE NOVEL

The transcendentalism in the book has led to two groundless charges by the critics, first that the book is atheistic, as expressed in the ideas of Jim Casy, and second that the book is collectivist, a code word meaning sympathetic to communism. These misreadings of the book grow out of an ignorance of transcendentalism and a misinterpretation of the call for unified action presented by the book.

The concept of the oversoul, in Emerson and in this book, is an affirmation of the universal presence of deity in all aspects of life. Emerson coined the term "oversoul" to express his understanding of the Christian tradition as he learned it from many Puritan sermons as well as from his reading of [Martin] Luther, [John] Calvin, Milton, and other theologians, as the literary historian Perry Miller has shown. Though Jim Casy probably had not read any works of theology, he does express the transcendental concept of the oversoul several times in the book in such language as this: "Maybe all men got one big soul ever'body's a part of." Transcendentalism has been criticized for its vagueness, but rightly or wrongly, it is an effort to assert that spiritual values are present in, and ultimately control, the material reality of the visible universe. It is clearly not the intent of Emerson nor of Jim Casy to deny the existence of deity. The charge of atheism is often made by those who say, "If you don't accept my definition of God, you must be an atheist." Neither Emerson nor Jim Casy would have agreed that they were atheists. . . .

NOT A COMMUNIST BOOK

Some would-be censors have mistakenly asserted that Steinbeck is sympathetic to communism. Steinbeck was in fact rather conservative; he supported the war in Vietnam, for example. His insistence in several works of fiction on the right of each person to his own piece of land can hardly be reconciled with communist tendencies toward collectivist forms of agriculture. However, Steinbeck's views outside the book are irrelevant to the implications of the symbols and actions in the book. It is clearly wrong to judge a book by the actual or assumed characteristics of the author.

The call for united action which runs through the book is not to be identified with the term "collectivist" as a synonym for communist. There is a tension between the individual and the group in the book, but its reconciliation is in the traditional Western world notion of the oneness of the humankind, as for example in the famous passage from [seventeenth-century British poet] John Donne, "Never send to know for whom the bell tolls, it tolls for thee."

The book calls for unified action that will preserve the right of farmers to their own farms, that will provide food for the hungry, that will subordinate the machine to the needs of the garden and to the needs of the human beings who toil in the garden. The book's call for unified action to meet the disasters of the 1930s is no more collectivist than was the action of the colonists who dumped the tea in Boston Harbor or who took up arms at Concord to fight the redcoats. There are many illustrations in the book of the need and ability of ordinary citizens to work together in solving problems, as for example when the migrants helped each other on the journey, or maintained order in the camp. This aspect of the novel is typical of American pragmatism—not of Marxist [referring to the philosophy of Karl Marx] ideas.

A TRUE CLASSIC

In the original meaning of the word, a classic is a book taught in the classroom. Steinbeck's book is certainly a classic in this sense of the word. As with a number of other classics, it is likely that many people read this book in high school. This use is appropriate because the book lends itself well to studying many aspects of American literature and life. *The Grapes of Wrath* won a Pulitzer prize in 1940 and is one of the major works of an American novelist who won the Nobel prize in 1962. It is difficult to understand how any American high school or college could forbid the teaching or use of the book while maintaining a claim to act as a proper agency for the education of the young in this democratic republic.

CHRONOLOGY

1902

Steinbeck born February 27 in Salinas, California

1905

Wright brothers' first airplane flight; Einstein publishes theory of relativity

1908

Steinbeck enters "Baby School"

1914

World War I begins; Panama Canal opens

1915

Einstein develops general theory of relativity; Steinbeck enters Salinas High School

1919

Treaty of Versailles end World War I; Steinbeck graduates from Salinas High School and enters Stanford University

1925

Steinbeck travels to New York City; works as a construction laborer and as a journalist for the *New York American*

1926

Steinbeck moves to Lake Tahoe, California, and works as a caretaker for a summer home

1929

Stock market crash; Hoover becomes president; Steinbeck publishes *Cup of gold*

1930

Marries Carol Henning; meets marine biologist and longtime friend Edward F. Ricketts

1932

Franklin Delano Roosevelt proposes the New Deal; dust bowl in the American Midwest begins; Steinbeck publishes *Pastures of Heaven*

1933

Hitler assumes power in Germany; Steinbeck publishes *To a God Unknown*

1934

Steinbeck's mother dies in February

1935

Tortilla Flat, Steinbeck's first major success, published by Covici-Friede; beginning of friendship with editor Pascal Covici

1936

Publishes *In Dubious Battle*; his father dies; publishes articles on migrants for *San Francisco News*

1937

Publishes *Of Mice and Men*; takes his first trip to Europe and Russia; publishes *The Red Pony*; opening of the play *Of Mice and Men*

1938

Publishes *The Long Valley* and *Their Blood Was Strong*; writes *The Grapes of Wrath* in one hundred days between June and October; buys ranch in Los Gatos; receives the New York Drama Critics Circle Award for the play *Of Mice and Men*

1939

World War II begins in Europe; Steinbeck publishes *The Grapes of Wrath*

1940

Steinbeck and Ricketts take research trip to the Sea of Cortez; Steinbeck wins the National Book Award and the Pulitzer Prize for *The Grapes of Wrath*; film versions of *The Grapes of Wrath* and *Of Mice and Men* released

1941

Japanese bomb Pearl Harbor; United States enters World War II; Steinbeck and Ricketts publish *The Sea of Cortez*

1942

Publishes *The Moon Is Down*; writes script for *Bombs Away: The Story of a Bomber Team*; Steinbeck and Carol Henning divorce; film of *Tortilla Flat* released

1943

Steinbeck marries Gwendolyn Conger; moves to New York; film of *The Moon Is Down* released; travels to Europe and North Africa as war correspondent for *New York Herald-Tribune*

1945

End of World War II; Publishes *Cannery Row*

1946

Beginning of the cold war between the United States and the USSR; Steinbeck's son John IV born

1947

Publishes *The Wayward Bus* and *The Pearl*; tours Russia with photographer Robert Capa

1948

Publishes *A Russian Journal*; elected to American Academy of Letters; film of *The Pearl* released; Ed Ricketts dies; Steinbeck and Gwendolyn Conger divorce

1950

Korean War begins; Publishes *Burning Bright*; opening of the play *Burning Bright*; writes script for *Viva Zapata!*; marries third wife, Elaine Scott

1951

Publishes *Log from the Sea of Cortez*

1952

Publishes *East of Eden*; film *Viva Zapata!* released

1954

Publishes *Sweet Thursday* (a sequel to *Cannery Row*)

1955

New York City opening of *Pipe Dream*, a Richard Rogers and Oscar Hammerstein III musical based on *Sweet Thursday*; Steinbeck purchases a summer home in Sag Harbor, Long Island; film of *East of Eden*, starring James Dean, released

1957

Publishes *The Short Reign of Pippin IV*; film of *The Wayward Bus* released

1958

Publishes *Once There Was a War*

1959

Travels in England and Wales, conducting research for a modern English version of Malory's *Morte d'Arthur*

1960

Travels across America with dog Charley

1961

John F. Kennedy becomes president; Steinbeck publishes *The Winter of Our Discontent*

1962

Cuban missile crisis; Publishes *Travels with Charley*; receives the Nobel Prize for Literature

1963

John F. Kennedy assassinated; Lyndon Johnson becomes president; Steinbeck travels to Scandinavia, Eastern Europe, and Russia

1965

Steinbeck covers the Vietnam War for Long Island *Newsday*

1966

Publishes *America and Americans*

1968

Martin Luther King Jr. assassinated; televised versions of *Travels with Charley, Of Mice and Men,* and *The Grapes of Wrath*; Steinbeck dies on December 20; buried in Salinas

1975

Publication of *Steinbeck: A Life in Letters,* edited by Elaine Steinbeck and Robert Wallsten

1989

Publication of *Working Days: The Journals of* The Grapes of Wrath, edited by Robert DeMott

1990

Frank Galati adapts and directs a dramatization of *The Grapes of Wrath*; Gary Sinise stars as Tom Joad

1991

Gallati's dramatization of *The Grapes of Wrath* wins New York Drama Critics Circle Award

1992

Film version of *Of Mice and Men* starring Gary Sinise and John Malkovich released

1993

Publication of Steinbeck's *Zapata: A Narrative in Dramatic Form on the Life of Emiliano Zapata*

FOR FURTHER RESEARCH

ABOUT JOHN STEINBECK

Jackson J. Benson, *The True Adventures of John Steinbeck, Writer.* New York: Viking, 1984.

Robert Murray Davis, ed., *Steinbeck: A Collection of Critical Essays.* Englewood Cliffs, NJ: Prentice-Hall, 1982.

John Ditsky, *John Steinbeck: Life, Work, and Criticism.* Fredericton, New Brunswick: York Press, 1985.

Thomas Fensch, ed., *Conversations with John Steinbeck.* Jackson: University Press of MIssissippi, 1988.

Warren French, *John Steinbeck.* New York: Grossett & Dunlap, 1961.

——, *John Steinbeck's Fiction Revisited.* New York: Twayne, 1994.

Tetsumaro Hayashi, *John Steinbeck: The Years of Greatness, 1936–1939.* Tuscaloosa: University of Alabama Press, 1993.

——, ed., *The Steinbeck Quarterly.* John Steinbeck Society of America. Ball State University, Muncie, IN, 47306.

Thomas Kiernan, *The Intricate Music: A Biography of John Steinbeck.* Boston: Little, Brown, 1979.

Peter Lisca, *John Steinbeck: Nature and Myth.* New York: Thomas Y. Crowell, 1978.

Jay Parini, *John Steinbeck: A Biography.* New York: Henry Holt, 1995.

Susan Shilligaw, ed., *The Steinbeck Newsletter.* Steinbeck Research Center. Available from San Jose State University, One Washington Square, 316 Wahlquist Library North, San Jose, CA 95192-0202. Founded 1987.

Elaine Steinbeck and Robert Wallsten, eds., *Steinbeck: A Life in Letters.* New York: Viking, 1975.

Clarice Swisher, ed., *Readings on John Steinbeck.* San Diego: Greenhaven Press, 1996.

E.W. Tedlock Jr. and C.V. Wicker, eds., *Steinbeck and His Critics: A Record of Twenty-Five Years.* Albuquerque: University of New Mexico Press, 1957.

ABOUT *THE GRAPES OF WRATH*

Harold Bloom, ed., *Modern Critical Interpretations of* The Grapes of Wrath. New York: Chelsea House, 1988.

Robert Con Davis, ed., *Twentieth Century Interpretations of* The Grapes of Wrath. Englewood Cliffs, NJ: Prentice-Hall, 1982.

Robert DeMott, ed., *Working Days: The Journals of* The Grapes of Wrath. New York: Viking, 1989.

John Ditsky, *Critical Essays on Steinbeck's* The Grapes of Wrath. Boston: G.K. Hall, 1989.

Agnes McNeill Donohue, ed., *A Casebook on* The Grapes of Wrath. New York: Thomas Y. Crowell, 1968.

Warren French, ed., *A Companion to* The Grapes of Wrath. New York: Viking, 1963.

The Grapes of Wrath. Playscript by Frank Galati. New York: Penguin, 1991.

Peter Lisca, ed., The Grapes of Wrath: *Text and Criticism.* New York: Viking, 1972.

Louis Owens, The Grapes of Wrath: *Trouble in the Promised Land.* Boston: Twayne, 1989.

David Wyatt, ed., *New Essays on* The Grapes of Wrath. New York: Cambridge University Press, 1990.

HISTORICAL BACKGROUND ON THE 1930S

Frederick Lewis Allen, *The Nineteen-Thirties in America, September 3, 1929–September 3, 1939.* New York: Harper & Brothers, 1940.

Fon Boardman Jr., *The Thirties: America and the Great Depression.* New York: Henry Z. Walck, 1967.

William Dudley, ed., *The Great Depression.* American History Series, ed. Teresa O'Neill. San Diego: Greenhaven Press, 1994.

Robert Goldston, *The Great Depression: The United States in the Thirties.* Indianapolis: Bobbs-Merrill, 1968.

Studs Terkel, *Hard Times: An Oral History of the Great Depression.* New York: Pantheon, 1970.

T.H. Watkins, *The Great Depression: America in the 1930s.* Boston: Little, Brown, 1993.

WORKS BY JOHN STEINBECK

Cup of Gold (1929)

Pastures of Heaven (1932)

To a God Unknown (1933)

Tortilla Flat (1935)

In Dubious Battle (1936)

"The Harvest Gypsies" (1936)

Of Mice and Men (1937)

The Long Valley (1938)

Their Blood Is Strong (1938)

The Grapes of Wrath (1939)

The Sea of Cortez (with Edward F. Ricketts) (1941)

The Moon Is Down (1942)

Bombs Away (1942)

Cannery Row (1945)

The Pearl (1947)

The Wayward Bus (1947)

A Russian Journal (1948)

Burning Bright (1950)

Log from the Sea of Cortez (1951)

East of Eden (1952)

Sweet Thursday (1954)

The Short Reign of Pippin IV (1957)

Once There Was a War (1958)

The Winter of Our Discontent (1961)

Travels with Charley in Search of America (1962)

America and Americans (1966)

Journal of a Novel: The "East of Eden" *Letters* (1969)

The Acts of King Arthur and His Noble Knights (1976)

Working Days: The Journals of The Grapes of Wrath (1989)

Zapata: A Narrative in Dramatic Form on the Life of Emiliano Zapata (1993)

INDEX